ELECTRONIC
JOURNALISM

ELECTRONIC JOURNALISM

WILLIAM A. WOOD

Columbia University Press

New York and London, 1967

William A. Wood is a professor in the Graduate School
of Journalism at Columbia University.

To LOUISA

PREFACE

Books which survey the field of electronic journalism are rare principally because they face a short life expectancy. The shape and the anatomy of broadcast news—particularly television news—keep changing. Anyone freezing the process in book form runs the risk that what he says today will not be true tomorrow.

I am taking the chance for two reasons. First, there ought to be a place in which the many aspects of the electronic news story are brought together instead of remaining fragmented in short pieces of writing appearing here and there in a variety of periodicals. Second, the first half of the 1960s brings us if not to an actual plateau in the development of the field, where for a while it will change less than previously, at least to a time when a number of recent milestones in the development of television news should be preserved while they are at hand and fresh in mind.

With electronic journalism as with any endeavor, be it farming, manufacturing, or practicing medicine, the final product that is visible is only the small part above the surface. Behind this product lie what are to the layman myriad mysterious and incredible skills, efforts, ingredients, and processes necessary to the final result. This is true of all the mass media, and of them all television involves the use of manpower and machinery least comprehensible to those not actually in the field. The jargon of the profession alone, to the uninitiated, sounds like a foreign tongue. In any respectable newsroom scarcely a sentence will be uttered all day long devoid of combinations of terms like cut-away, line-up, stand-upper, lead-in, VTR, mag track, pad, double chain, lab time, voice over, lap, and speed.

I hope that this book will make some of this complicated business a little less mysterious to the general reader and will still be of service to the professional in evaluating the status of his calling and in explaining at both national and local levels the whys and wherefores and the philosophies behind the final product—news on the air. I have attempted to do this in terms that everybody can understand. If I am, in a way, "of" the broadcast news world by background, I am also "of" the academic world in a rather practical way, teaching in a school of journalism. A teacher must know how to get through to students, many of whom are unfamiliar with his field, and it is my intention to bring that kind of know-how to this book.

Most of the emphasis is on television. This is not to imply that radio has lost its importance as a source of news, but I do not believe a book of this kind can do justice to two media. Television has been selected because of its enormous potential and because these are its critical and formative years.

Readers will find this book for the most part a favorable report on television journalism and on the men responsible for it because I sincerely believe that a favorable report is merited. I believe also that all television is adversely criticized beyond what is fair by newspaper and magazine columnists and by observers of the social and cultural habits of the American people. What I consider to be the prejudice or self-serving of such fault-finders extends even to the news and public affairs area of television where, if any place, television rates good marks. So I am giving it good marks.

I want to express my gratitude to the network and station newsmen and executives, to the librarians of the Television Information Office of the National Association of Broadcasters, and to private individuals for providing me with background and other material essential to the writing of this book.

July, 1967   WILLIAM A. WOOD

CONTENTS

ONE

TELEVISION—
INDISPENSABLE
MEDIUM
FOR NEWS

In Boston, Massachusetts, there is a television station affiliated with the National Broadcasting Company which
broadcasts a local half-hour news program every weekday
at noon. This program has a substantially larger audience
than the soap opera offered at the same time on the rival
station of the Columbia Broadcasting System.

It is not only by chance that this news program outdraws
a particularly hypnotic form of television escapism. It is by
virtue of the attainment by the television newsman—the
electronic journalist—of a noteworthy degree of professionalism and command of the tools of his trade, and the
recognition of this by the viewers. In fact, it is the premise
set forth in the opening chapter of this book that the evolu-
tion of the television journalist has reached a point where
he even outperforms the competition in his own field, the
medium of news, so that to a majority of Americans he has
become the most important single news voice of them all.

The men and the business of journalism are rarely news
in themselves; but certainly the great events of the 1960s

which go down in history will have to include the emergence of the power of television as a disseminator of those events through electronic journalism, to exert an impact on the American public over a range we can only now begin to assess.

A number of factors are relevant to this story: the nature and scope of the news itself in the decade of the sixties; the expansion and maturing of television as a journalistic medium; active interest in television's affairs on the part of an agency of the federal government; and the attitudes and behavior of the television audience. Each of them plays a role in the drama.

The Nixon versus Kennedy campaign for the presidency in 1960 and Kennedy's subsequent election ushered in a period of dramatic news events at home and all around the world. These were clearly of great contemporary and historic significance to America and Americans, and the public recognized them for what they were. We were confronted with a Cuban crisis, and bloodied in our increasing involvement in Asia. We were privy to the suspenseful competition with the Soviet Union for superiority in space. We witnessed the emergence of civil rights for the Negro as a domestic issue with an emotional impact unequaled since the Civil War. We experienced the shattering assassination of a President, and his somber funeral. And our hearts were touched by another solemn ceremony across the sea when Winston Churchill died. These were moving and exciting times for those who followed the news, and challenging times for those who reported the news.

Coincidentally, the commercial television industry in the United States attacked, with a real explosion of men and muscle, the problem of fashioning its medium into a first-class, professional purveyor of news. The motivation for

INDISPENSABLE MEDIUM FOR NEWS

this came from one or a combination of the needs of the times, the broadcaster's sense of responsibility, competition within the industry or pressure from Washington. In 1961, Chairman Newton Minow of the Federal Communications Commission (FCC) laid the accusation of "vast wasteland" on commercial television's doorstep, raising the specter of FCC action in the area of program content, a possibility broadcasters have fought tooth and nail for a long time. To what degreee, if any, the Chairman's chastisement of the medium stimulated change remains an unsettled question. In any case, since Minow spoke, the non-wasteland —the news—can show a steady record of progress.

The burgeoning of news first became evident at the national network level. ABC, CBS, and NBC commenced to devote considerably more attention than before and on a higher professional plane to the big national and world stories of the day. Competition, which had always been keen among the networks for the entertainment audience, now took on almost equal intensity in news programming. As NBC's former President and Board Chairman, Robert Kintner, described it in the early sixties, "The rivalry among the networks has an intensity that has not been seen in American journalism since the days of Hearst and Pulitzer." This spirit was caught by local television stations, and out of it more and higher caliber news became available to viewers.

The most memorable examples of this expansion were in the category of live, national coverage of major events —space shots, election nights, United Nations crises— which followed seemingly one on top of the other with all their immediacy, color, and drama. Equally important was the breakthrough in regular news programs in 1963. NBC and then CBS escalated their prestigious evening news shows from a quarter to a half hour, and the chain reaction which followed brought news time, both national and local, to a new high.

With an endless stream of news being made and a greatly expanded facility in television to report it, the American people lost no time in tuning in. All television programming was holding its own in audience figures, but news did better than that.

The number of homes owning television sets went from 45.2 million in 1960 to 58.6 million in 1966, meaning more potential viewers. Overall television viewing time per viewer remained constant. Surveys in 1967 indicated the average viewer spent three and a half hours per day watching. Regular daily news programs showed a steady growth in audience each year after 1959. Some of the figures were impressive even by entertainment program standards. NBC claimed a nightly audience of 18,540,000 for the Huntley-Brinkley show. CBS cited 16,730,000 for The Evening News with Walter Cronkite. Local news programs, produced by individual stations, achieved comparable popularity. In Los Angeles, NBC found it necessary to schedule The Huntley-Brinkley Report directly opposite KNXT's (CBS) locally produced The Big News in an attempt to dent the local program's top audience rating in that area. During the same year, the noon news half hour on WBZ-TV, Boston, became David to the Goliath of soap opera on CBS. It is not surprising that this audience behavior should show up in some measurable way.

In fact, in 1964 a national survey conducted by Elmo Roper and Associates[1] showed that the public gets most of its news from television. Two subsequent surveys—a national study by Sindlinger and one for the Texas area by

Joe Belden Associates—confirmed the finding. Through annual studies beginning in 1959, Roper found that television's competitive position vis-à-vis daily newspapers improved each year, and that since 1963 television has been in the lead as a news source. Even if this last proposition can be debated, there is no disputing the fact that the trend is steadily upward. A companion finding of Roper's, which tells much about the growing maturity and professionalism of television in the eyes of the public, is that people give television the highest rating for credibility of all the mass media.

A fact that lends weight to the thesis that television news enjoys top status with viewers is the rush of commercial sponsors to such programming. Some kinds of sponsors gravitate to news for purposes of prestige and image; others want the chance for constant repetition of their message that can be provided by programs the audience tunes back to day after day. But most advertisers are cold, practical people, and the fact that they wait in line to buy a spot on the regular news and pay a premium for it, and that some of them will invest heavily in a live special event telecast or put their names on an instant news special or a documentary, indicates that the audience is there, presumably in a receptive and attentive mood.

Keeping an eye on these developments are the editors and publishers of electronic journalism's oldest competitor, the newspapers. For years the leaders of the print media have been concerned over the real competition that broadcasting has presented for the advertising dollar. But they have been a little contemptuous of television's news product. Now, however, they have begun to grant respect, sometimes reluctantly, sometimes willingly, to the electronic news performance and the hold it has gained on its audience. At one of the meeting grounds of newspaper and broadcast reporters, the news conference, a telling point is who asks the questions. Traditionally, press reporters dominated the questioning. When broadcasters tried their hand at it, they tended to show their ignorance. But with the 1960s broadcasters began to show their mettle. Newspaper and wire service reporters took notes. It didn't matter to them who asked the questions as long as they were the right ones. And with more experienced, higher-quality newsmen, the broadcast organizations were asking the right ones.

The surest indication that newspapermen see broadcasting, particularly television, as a strong competitor for the news audience, is the hard look many of them are taking at their own product, and the changes some of the most progressive of them are making in it. John H. Murphy, Executive Director of the Texas Daily Newspaper Association, reflects this attitude of self-examination when he says, "The attitude of people towards newspapers is one of decreasing interest . . . there seems to be little doubt about the need for more information about what people want in their newspapers. We need to have—and our editors need to accept—much more knowledge about the people who make up our present audience and our potential audience." [2] Changes have already been introduced in papers like the *Chicago Daily News* and the *St. Louis Globe Democrat*, as well as the *New York Herald Tribune* before its demise. These innovations include a different layout, a more exciting look, more columns, more treatment in depth, more analyses. Erwin Canham, Editor of the *Christian Science Monitor*, has changed the make-up and editorial style of his distinguished publication to accommodate to what he sees as the rising role of radio and television in swift handling of news in depth as well as spot news. He says: "The press needs this different treatment to compete with the speed and vividness" of the broadcast media.

Whether for reasons of diversification or "life insurance," newspaper organizations are now the owners of over 170 television stations in the country. And some of the latter are giving their press colleagues a real run for their money in the news sector.

Television has some limitations the press does not have, but television has a natural attribute that is recognized though not completely understood—the peculiarly personal and graphic impact on its viewers which the printed word cannot match. This close relationship with the audience is not by any means confined to entertainment television, but occurs just as strongly if not more so in journalistic television. Television comes closest to putting the audience physically at the scene of the event. It's at its best as a transmitter of experience. There are elements of emotion and of involvement in television's chemistry. The involvement does not insure that the viewer will be informed and enlightened by what he sees and hears. But it does provide the broadcast journalist with a potent catalyst for drawing and holding his audience, toward the end of informing and enlightening it. The rapport between reporter and viewer is almost total. Television newsmen with large followings, like Walter Cronkite, are made newly aware of this every day, and they are awed by its ultimate consequence. As with the *New York Times*, "The *Times* said it; it must be true"—it is now, "Walter said it; it must be true."

The magnetic forces that come into play in television journalism probably have their greatest impact on one particular segment of American society—what might be called the nonreader segment. Newspaper editors are familiar with nonreaders—those who peruse the headlines, sports, comics, advertisments, and bother with nothing else. In turn, they are recognized by television news directors, who have been around long enough to know their audiences, as a significant part of their viewership— a group large enough in itself to give television an edge as the leading news medium for most people. These nonreading viewers expose themselves to an amount of news on television that they would seldom absorb as newspaper readers. In much of its news coverage television cannot be comprehensive, but—unfortunate as it may be—the news which television airs may be accepted and deemed sufficient by the nonreader.

The most striking evidence that television in the United States has emerged as a journalistic force second to none is the effect it has on the course of major issues and events. This book will consider later on the phenomenon of television as a participant in the news, as a formulator and crystallizer of opinion on national and world issues. The universal appeal and the universal presence of the medium can turn a civil rights struggle, a war in Vietnam, or a presidential burial into a common experience for viewers in Bangor, Oklahoma City, and Grand Rapids. We are a populous, diverse, and complex nation. But today Americans are being brought together, informed, consulted, surveyed, convinced, repelled, moved, and argued with in a way that was never before possible, not even in the days of the birth of our nation. And television is doing it.

TWO

FROM
CRYSTAL SET
TO COLOR
TELEVISION

In considering the history of broadcasting from 1920 to the present, it is important to keep in mind that the product made available to mankind was quite different from that offered by newspapers when they were born. Newspapers have always placed primary dependence for their circulation—their means of economic support—on the news. Radio and later television built their audiences primarily on entertainment, and for the most part they depend on this as their base today. Throughout the half century of its development, electronic journalism has been an adjunct of its medium, not the prime concern. The advances it has made during this comparatively short period must be considered against that central fact.

This is not to say that the early pioneers in radio failed to use broadcasting's obvious attributes—speed and presence on the scene—in covering the events and happenings of their time for the crystal set audience. History records that from the very first, informational programs were carried on the air. It is significant that with all the glamorous history of entertainment programming, the milestones that stand out along the road relate to broadcasting's role in transmitting the events of these news-filled decades.

When one of the very early stations (KDKA, Pittsburgh) was licensed in 1920, it treated its listeners to the Harding-Cox presidential election returns. The first linking up of two stations (WEAF, New York and WNAC, Boston in 1923) was used to carry a football game. Later that year the scattering of people with home radio sets heard President Calvin Coolidge's message to Congress. Silent Cal figured in another radio first; his was the first inaugural reported over the air in 1925 on a hook-up that covered twenty cities. The very first coast-to-coast program was the Rose Bowl football game broadcast from Pasadena on New Year's day, 1927.

So it was public events, including sports, that were in the vanguard of radio's early interest in contemporary affairs. These were to continue to receive attention through the period of radio's growth, and extend into the early years of television.

The development of the routine daily news program on radio was slow by comparison. For a number of years, daily news broadcasting was undistinguished. Radio had few trained newsmen at its command and no means of gathering the news on a regular basis. At first, announcers pirated stories and read them on the air direct from the daily press. Later, the stations and the newly formed national networks (NBC in 1926, CBS a year later) purchased the wire services of Associated Press, United Press, and International News Service. Many used them verbat'm in broadcasts of what was known as the rip-and-read era.

Newspapers observed what was going on, and became worried about radio as a competitor in the newspapers' own bailiwick. In the early thirties the national depression arrived, and the papers forced the wires to discontinue selling their services to broadcasters. The ensuing freeze lasted from 1933 to 1938, and accelerated a trend on the part of both NBC and CBS to go about building their own news-gathering organizations and staffs, which formed the base of the big broadcast news organizations of today. A related event generated what was to grow to striking proportions in radio and particularly in television—the use of the news personality.

By 1933 the networks were giving the name "commentator" to newspaper-trained men like Boake Carter, H. V. Kaltenborn, Lowell Thomas, and Walter Winchell, and putting them on the air to interpret the news. They won rapid public acceptance, and a star system was born in electronic news. During the thirties the number of commentators on CBS and on NBC's two networks (called the Red and the Blue) rose from six to twenty in number.

Here and there a few correspondents represented the networks abroad, and by the early thirties reported more or less regularly to the American audience. The wire service freeze encouraged cautious expansion of this select corps. The event which dramatized this dimension in radio news came in 1937 when H. V. Kaltenborn reported the Spanish Civil War from the battle front. By this same year, Edward R. Murrow as European correspondent for CBS began to gather the nucleus of an overseas staff. Max Jordan was busy with the same job for NBC. A new radio network—Mutual—entered the field with a serious interest in news. It was March 13, 1938 when CBS broadcast its first World News Roundup, using correspondents from various European cities. This was the forerunner of what was to become a radio news standard.

In the fall of 1938 the Munich crisis signaled the ominous likelihood of world war. Radio's technical facilities and manpower were marshaled just in time to bring first hand the dramatic twenty days between September 10 and 29 —culminating in the betrayal of Czechoslovakia for "peace in our time"—to a breathless American listening audience. Through literally hundreds of broadcasts, the small network of overseas staffs were stretched to the limit in delivering the running story, bringing reporters' voices direct from the European cities involved and the voices of Hitler, Chamberlain, Benes, Mussolini, Goebbels, and Pope Pius.

When war came, and especially by the time that the United States entered it, radio was ready. NBC's Blue network had become the American Broadcasting Company. An army of network correspondents, along with armed services reporters in all war theaters and dozens of news commentators at home, backed by closely coordinated facilities and manpower of the four networks, tackled the long, four-year assignment. The speed, the personalness, and the you-are-there qualities of the medium had never before been so dramatically illustrated, or been proven to be so necessary to the American people.

Radio correspondents accompanying the men at war gave as little concern to personal safety as their print media comrades in this and other wars. A new roll call of names became household words to listeners. In addition to Murrow, Max Jordan, and William L. Shirer, there were Morgan Beatty, Winston Burdett, Upton Close, Charles Collingwood, Elmer Davis, Bill Downs, Joseph C. Harsch, Quincy Howe, John B. Hughes, Fulton Lewis, Merrill Mueller, Eric Sevareid, Howard K. Smith, and Lowell Thomas, all of whom were to move on to eminent positions in the broadcast news profession once hostilities ended.

Documentary, background, and feature programs grew up alongside the hard news and commentary. Programs like The Man Behind the Gun, The Army Hour, The Navy Hour, were becoming prominent. It was the first "radio war." The Korean War, and later the Vietnam conflict, were to be known as "television wars."

By the time the tide turned in favor of the Allies, the worldwide system of American radio with experience gained in the crucible, fielded a full-fledged human and electronic organization for the landings in Europe on D Day, the reconquest of the Philippines, the fall of Germany, and the surrender of the Japanese on the battleship *Missouri* in Tokyo Bay. Television with its great potential as a news medium was about to spring half-grown from the forehead of its sire, and World War II was to be radio's hour of greatness in the light of history.

The inevitable period of anticlimax followed V-J Day, with the men who fought the war, with the people of the United States, and with the combat-geared news organizations of broadcasting. Radio demobilized as did everyone else. But left behind was a dedication of airtime to regular news programs at a level which was well above the prewar level, and an audience whose appetite had been whetted for news on the air, so that radio news was destined to retain a strong position in the program schedules of networks and of the better stations to this day.

This all too brief account of the history of radio in a book primarily about television journalism is essential, because the latter form grew from its audio predecessor and profited in many ways from what had been learned the hard way by the first of the electronic media. The newsmen with the glamorous, new instrument owe an eternal debt to their brethren of the thirties and forties.

Television made its appearance officially as early as 1939, when on the 30th of April that year Franklin D. Roosevelt was televised live at the opening of the New York World's Fair. During that year NBC established a regular television service, i.e., two evening programs a week, each one hour long. Its audience in the New York area was reached through 150 receiving sets. For television firsts, there were the telecasts of a major league baseball game, a college baseball game from Columbia University's Baker Field, and a professional fight.

By May of 1942 there were just ten commercial television stations on the air; only six of them continued to provide service during the war, and the available audience was tiny. Altogether there were only about 8,000 television receivers extant, mostly in the homes of television company officials and engineers.

For all practical purposes, television got its start in the years following World War II. It began to mature in the postwar world, a world of the atomic bomb, a world recovering from a vast conflagration, and a world facing great political and social change. Television was to become —from its small beginnings in 1945 and earlier—the new communicator to chronicle the human story in the postwar period.

As with radio before it, the special event drew most of television's first interest in the area of news and public affairs, while the backbone of entertainment—as with radio—was hardening into the primary program pattern. Films of events at the war's end were widely shown by existing television stations: V-E Day, the ceremonies on the *Missouri*, Eisenhower's return to New York. Late in 1945 the very first Macy's Thanksgiving Day Parade was telecast. An early meeting of the United Nations Security

Council was covered the following year. In 1947 CBS carried a nine-part film series on the atom bomb tests at Bikini in the Pacific. That same year President Harry S. Truman's address to a joint session of Congress was picked up, and later the first telecast of a presidential talk directly from the White House pointed the new direction—the HST version of FDR's radio fireside chats.

The 1948 national political conventions in Philadelphia were the first ones to get real television coverage. We were still three years away from coast-to-coast network linkups, but airborne relays carried the conventions to the Pacific, and it was estimated that between ten and twelve million people were able to watch. A CBS historian said of this coverage: "Television and its performance constituted the most important fact about the 1948 political conventions. It was something new in the experience of the delegates. And it was something new for the American people." Here was early evidence that television in its journalistic role was going to have an influence of a new order of magnitude over the media which came before it.

Mr. Truman was the surprise winner in the 1948 election, and among other things won himself the honor of being the first President whose inaugural was both heard and seen on the air.

In 1950 came the war in Korea. In a much smaller focus it gave television news the chance to prove itself that radio had had in World War II. The television film cameras were there to see, to hear, to report to the American people.

The early fifties saw a new and significant use for television's cameras—Senate hearings. Estes Kefauver suddenly became nationally known as cameras focused on him and on the hands of his star witness, Frank Costello. This was in

1951. In 1954 Senator Joseph McCarthy faced lawyer Joseph Welch at what was known as the Army-McCarthy Hearings, and the cameras gave the people an opportunity to judge for themselves what the hue and cry was all about. Senator John L. McClellan's racket hearings were covered in 1957, and with television an established instrument for putting the American audience in the very hearing room, it has since become a regular adjunct of any respectable senate committee inquiry—notably J. William Fulbright's Foreign Relations Committee examination of Vietnam in 1965 and 1966.

The political conventions of 1952 and 1956 were given the unprecedented attention that experience and more sophisticated television equipment systems made possible, and they enjoyed the advantage of instant nationwide dissemination, since the coast-to-coast link of coaxial cable and microwave relay had been completed in 1951. In 1956 at Chicago, Chet Huntley first worked in tandem with David Brinkley for NBC, and a chemical reaction occurred which was to affect television journalism profoundly.

In the first years after World War II, news programming on a regularly scheduled basis was spotty and experimental. The networks were waiting for more television homes and more cities on the network line. By 1949 the FCC reported 101 stations on the air in 59 cities and 26 cities linked by cable, and in that year the television leaders got down to serious business with news. John Cameron Swayzee began his long tenure as proprietor of the NBC Camel News Caravan; Douglas Edwards did likewise on Douglas Edwards with the News. WABD, the DuMont station in New York, and the Daily News Station, WPIX, did regular newscasting. All these programs had commercial sponsors. Earlier the broadcasters had to sustain such programs with little financial support.

In 1950, television audiences saw the face, or many faces, of war in Korea on the daily news programs. Seeing film shot on the scene as well as hearing this kind of news gave a new impact to the story and suggested to the war correspondents and the newsrooms at home the magnitude of their responsibility as journalists. Other stories in the early fifties tested broadcast journalism's skills, exposing audiences to this medium of experience. These included the multimillion-dollar Brinks robbery in Boston, the incident at Blair House when two Puerto Ricans tried to kill President Truman, the Japanese Peace Treaty proceedings, nuclear bomb tests at Eniwetok, and Nasser's seizure of power in Egypt.

From 1951, when NBC and CBS evening news shows were able to reach the entire country, New York and other network-affiliated stations began to air their own local versions of television news. Fifteen-minute (and a few half-hour) programs with news, features, and sports were scheduled adjacent to the fifteen-minute network programs. In 1955 John Daly joined ABC News, and made it a Daly-Swayzee-Edwards threesome each evening in many cities.

In 1956 the spirit of competition among the networks in the television news area intensified. Tired of being rated second in quality to CBS, NBC began to do something about it. Late in the year, they replaced Swayzee on their prestige evening news show with the team of Huntley and Brinkley, which had done so well at the conventions. And Chet and David gave a new look and sound to NBC news audiences.

All three networks concurrently increased their use of

news film and replaced announcers with "on the air" newsmen. And as seems so often to have happened in the development of television, just as they were ready for more demanding news work, a demanding story came along— Little Rock in 1957. This was the beginning of television's decade of coverage of the struggle for Negro rights, which coverage itself was to play a role in the outcome.

National and world stories for television's mill kept coming in the late fifties. The first U. S. satellite was put into orbit; both Queen Elizabeth and Nikita Khrushchev visited America; Vice President Nixon shook up the comrades during a trip to the Soviet Union; Eisenhower traveled abroad too. Fidel Castro came to power in Cuba. And television news was there. By now CBS News was fighting to keep up with NBC News, and in 1958 they pitted Walter Cronkite against the Huntley-Brinkley team.

There was another form of journalism in which television was to involve itself but which emerged more slowly than either of those discussed above—the in-depth program, the special, the documentary. This form was borrowed from radio, from film, and from the theater, and eventually it came to have some characteristics of its own. Ed Murrow and Fred Friendly of CBS had done some imaginative work in radio with Hear It Now, and they were among the pioneers in adapting this idea to the sight medium.

In the early 1950s See It Now demonstrated on its first outing the technical magic of television by showing live in one picture the waters of the Atlantic and Pacific Oceans to a bemused audience. But it went on to demonstrate more intellectual matters concerning the problems and issues of our times, to show how television could be much more than just a picture. Christmas with the troops on the front lines in Korea will never be forgotten by those who saw it. A See It Now which revealed Senator McCarthy for what he was, largely by playing back McCarthy from film, stirred up a storm and as a result brought McCarthy equal air time, which didn't appear to do for the Senator what he had hoped.

A weekly program, Outlook—later Chet Huntley Reporting—went on NBC in 1956. David Brinkley's Journal came along in 1961.

The idea of the press conference on the air was brought to reality as early as 1948 with the Martha Rountree-Lawrence Spivak Meet the Press program, in which NBC newsmen questioned prominent public men and women. CBS countered with Man of the Week (now Face the Nation) in 1952. Between them these two programs have had nearly every national and world leader—including Chairman Nikita Khrushchev—as guests, and the format has been borrowed by many other network and local programs.

A new era in news documentaries began on all three networks in 1959. Eyewitness to History (a weekly), FYI, CBS Reports (the successor to See It Now), NBC White Paper, ABC Focus, Project 20, and 20th Century came to the television screen. The "instant special" also made its appearance in what was an enlightened sponsor's contribution to expanding television news service to the public. The Gulf Oil Company arranged with NBC News to pay for fast-breaking news coverage on television to be produced and scheduled at the discretion of NBC news executives.

"News to get up by" would hardly have seemed television's cup of tea in the fifties, but some workmanlike programs produced by overnight staffs are now offered in the 7 to 9 A.M. period, including the phenomenally successful Today show on NBC. Today has been on the air five days a week for 15 years, along with news segments in its two-hour length. It has interviews and discussions with officials and opinion leaders which give depth to the news and have made the program "required watching" in Washington.

The contest for the presidency in 1960 saw an innovation in political broadcasting. Television played the communicator's role between candidates and voters in the debates between Kennedy and Nixon. Whether they should be called debates or confrontations or simply joint appearances on the air, each program of the series was viewed by 65 to 70 million Americans, and probably helped tip the scales for Kennedy, who made a better impression on most viewers than did his adversary.

By that time, the United States was on the threshold of color television, which would soon become one of the many notable milestones the medium recorded in the span of its first twenty years. Our history lesson stops deliberately at the year 1960 because the remainder of this book deals with the period of the 1960s, the most important part of the story of television journalism. In 1960, according to the FCC, there were 559 stations in the country and 52 million television sets, reaching 112 million viewers. As this book goes to press, U. S. television has 732 stations and 177.28 million viewers. The steady expansion of television and its audience in six years undoubtedly bears a relationship to television's arrival as a first-rank communicator of the story of our times and our world.

THREE

NEWS
AS IT IS
HAPPENING

The historical review in the preceding chapter touched upon three forms of electronic journalism: the live program; the regularly scheduled news program; and the in-depth program. Let us now consider each of these forms in its contemporary manifestations and add a fourth form, the editorial, which played little part as a broadcast form until the sixties.

The live form as discussed here means the extended coverage of a story, in which all or a large part of the story is transmitted as it is taking place. This coverage may be direct from the scene as it happens, or it may be delayed by time for film shipment. The Rose Bowl game is instantaneous, while much of the funeral ceremonies of Winston Churchill were delayed for the time it took to fly the film from Britain. The coverage can be from the studio, as in the case of reporting election returns or in an emergency such as a power blackout or a hurricane. Obviously, the live story can be classified in another way, namely as the story that may be planned, such as a presidential inauguration, or one that is not planable, such as the Kennedy assassination.

In its live form, television leads from its greatest natural strength. It takes you there. You are an eyewitness as well as an earwitness as the news is happening. There is a freshness and excitement to it. No one has put it better than Theodore H. White, author of two superb books on presidential election campaigns. "Television has erased the filter of time: one sees the event in the now, in all its stunning immediacy, without the overnight filter that the morning newspapers once provided." [1]

It was more than chance that the first program to reach the whole country when the last transcontinental microwave links were completed in 1951 was the Japanese Peace Treaty Conference, live from the San Francisco Opera House. It was a recognition of television's responsibility to transmit an important story and of television's arresting power in its live form. Every year since has seen live programming which, aided by technical developments and expanded physical facilities plus a growing news corps of men learning by their experience, has provided more deft service to the viewing public. A measure of the progress made through fifteen years of nationwide television was the handling of the Kennedy assassination story in November, 1963. During those four shattering days, the American people were there to see and mourn. Television had reached a new level of performance that could stand a stern test.

Very early in the game, television and the politician realized they were made for each other, and by now national politics biennially eats up goodly chunks of television time, the most dramatic part of which is broadcast live. In 1960 and 1964, when certain primary races held more than usual interest and political significance, television networks threw money and manpower into covering the story. The Kennedy versus Humphrey contests in Wisconsin and West Virginia and the battles among Goldwater, Rockefeller, and Lodge in New Hampshire, Oregon, and California involved constant network film crew attention, airtime beyond the regular news programs, and special programs to report the outcome of the vote and to interpret the results.

The national conventions of the major political parties have received a more streamlined television treatment in recent years, owing to changes made by the parties themselves to meet electronic criteria, but that treatment is no less massive. In 1960, the three networks spent a total of $5 million on the two conclaves, and in 1964 the cost tripled. To provide the audience with the many faces of the quadrennial saga, the network anchormen now have access to as many as 250 reporters, the behind-the-scenes news producers and directors of the extravaganza can choose from the battery of television monitors up to sixty locations from which they can deliver live picture and sound. With their small and highly portable cameras there is almost no place the rules permit them to go that they can't take the viewer. All of this hardware and mobility gave to the drama of the Kennedy nomination in Los Angeles in 1960 and the Goldwater nomination in San Francisco four years later their moments of fascinating watching.

The campaigns which followed—in 1960 the battle royal between John F. Kennedy and Richard Nixon, and in 1964 between Lyndon Johnson and Barry Goldwater—commanded again more live attention. Live broadcasts, when combined with the unfolding political story on regular news programs and the time bought and used by the two major parties to sell their candidates, showed, if any doubt remained, that television has become the politico's indispensable campaign instrument and the public's means of seeing the events "in the now."

In the reporting of election returns lies the most arresting innovation in the political story of the sixties. In 1964, broadcasting made its largest contribution in this area. The networks had been striving individually for years to narrow the gap between television's instant reporting capability and the time necessary to collect and total the vote. After a pioneering period of experiment with coveys of hired precinct reporters, data computers, and systems of projecting outcomes from samples, a dramatic culmination came about in 1964 with a far-ranging, centralized recording and predicting system which proved itself the first time it was tried.

ABC, CBS, and NBC, with the later addition of the two national press wire services, Associated Press and United Press International—pooled their efforts to produce a nationwide system for gathering and processing election returns. The speed which resulted made possible the naming of Lyndon Johnson as winner for the presidency even before the polls had closed in the Far West. And races at all levels were for the most part called and correctly called within two or three hours after voting ended. The demands implicit in the idea of live coverage—news-right-now—had changed a whole era in national political reporting. The traditional night-long vigil to learn the winner was at an end.

The National Election Service, as it was called, employed 75,000 temporary reporters, and cost nearly $2 million, which was far less than an aggregate of individual network efforts would have been; and this saving and other practical considerations insure that the National Election Service will be the standard election reporting system, permanently.

The election process is only the beginning of life in the television fishbowl for our public officials. Television has become the vehicle for direct, daily contact between the people and the government, at the municipal, state, and federal level. In the live event form, this includes the important pronouncement by the president, the governor, or the mayor; the news conference; the public address, the sit-down-and-talk-it-over policy examination known in FDR's day as the Fireside Chat.

National crises particularly have underscored the live use of electronic communication. Presidents Eisenhower, Kennedy, and Johnson took to radio and television without delay during critical times like the U-2 incident, the Cuba missile affair, and the escalation of fighting in Vietnam. State and city chief executives do likewise when emergency situations warrant it. Broadcasters have a good record for contributing facilities and airtime to make such instant communication possible.

In the legislative branch of the government, the most prevalent form of government in action over television continues to be the congressional hearing, the most notable recent example being the Senate Foreign Relations Committee examination of our policies in Vietnam. At this writing, television and radio are still excluded from the formal sessions of the full House and Senate. But access has been granted by a number of state legislatures and other governmental bodies below the federal level, and the opening up of chambers on Capitol Hill would seem to be only a matter of time.

As for the judiciary, television and the courts of justice are a story all their own, a complex one which will be discussed later on.

Alan Shepard's flight, May 5, 1961, launched the exciting continuing story of man in space. Television was there, and television has been there ever since. The American people have gotten to know a growing number of space heroes almost as well as if they lived next door, and in the course of hundreds of air hours, the people have accumulated knowledge of the rudiments of space science—television being for many of them nearly their only source of such knowledge.

From the Shepard flight to and including the Stafford-Cernan flight in 1966, the networks have devoted hundreds of hours to live coverage of space events. By the time of our spaceman voyage to the moon, viewers may also see the climax of that story live. The networks have already requested room on the space ship for a television camera.

Audiences have been witness to television's technical progress in the picture coverage of the space story. The live audio with pictures later from the scene of the crucial splash down of a manned flight, was replaced by instantaneous picture and sound on June 6, 1966 with the return of Tom Stafford and Gene Cernan in Gemini 9. It was another development of the space age that made this possible—the orbiting communications satellite. Television transmission requires a line-of-sight between sending and receiving points. A recovery scene, far at sea, is over the edge of the earth and out of visual reach without a relay point which is in line of sight of both sender and receiver. The satellite provides that relay.

It takes no great imagination to foresee what communications relays in space mean to television, and particularly live television. The satellite or a combination of satellites is technically capable of relaying picture and sound from any given point on earth to any other point; thus, live presentation of an event from anywhere to the rest of the world is possible. The year 1963 marked the first use of such a satellite; since then portions of the Churchill funeral rites, the Olympic games from Tokyo, and many other programs have been broadcast live. One form tried out with some success is the two-way or three-way special which brings world statesmen together in extemporaneous discussion, each speaking from his own country. For all intents and purposes, they are in the same room. This has, to say the least, interesting implications.

Pending the resolution of jurisdictional and cost problems related to intercontinental transmission and the accessibility of more satellites, "live television delayed" (prerecording on film or video tape) remains an important instrument for intercontinental stories in the sixties. The Churchill funeral has been mentioned. The revolt in the Dominican Republic and some of the Cuban stories are others. The visit of Pope Paul to New York reached United States audiences instantaneously, but it was seen delayed by viewers in Europe and elsewhere. On-the-spot coverage on that day, October 4, 1965, was a notable example of the ubiquity of television.

The Pope's itinerary called for a full schedule of activities all over the city—a mass at St. Patrick's Cathedral, a speech before the United Nations, a giant rally in Yankee Stadium. By pooling their men and resources, the three networks managed to be everywhere he was from the time he put down at Kennedy airport until he flew off from Kennedy fourteen hours later. Ninety cameras were used, spotted all over the city. A corps of newsmen and

27

church personnel did the reporting and commentary. CBS, which handled the first leg of the pool for all networks and New York stations, used 26 camera locations to cover the motor trip of His Eminence from Kennedy airport to St. Patrick's—one in a hovering helicopter, one in the airport control tower, one each in mobile units running just ahead of and just behind the Pope's car, and the rest on rooftops, giant cranes, fork-lifts, and in parks and terraces along the parade route. The eminent visitor was not out of the sight of millions of viewers for even a moment on the entire 24-mile trip.

Two phenomena of the sixties have a bearing on live television and deserve mention here. One is the arrival of color television; the other is the televising of sports. Are sports events news? You would, of course, have a hard time convincing a large part of the population that they are not. Sports events have been program ammunition since broadcasting began, but in the past several years they have come into their own as a big and lucrative occupier of television time. Technically, play-by-play has reached a high degree of pictorial perfection, and as with the newspaper, television fields some of the most articulate ad libbers and commentators in this category of journalism. As it has done with the more orthodox news event, live television is providing a wide audience with new knowledge of a variety of sports. In its restless search for more and more fodder to feed the demand, television has made of the football and baseball fan an armchair expert on everything from water skiing to jai alai. Golf must have attained the peak of its popularity through the fond attention television has been giving it.

Today the only artificiality about the television picture —its black and whiteness—is being eliminated. After several years during which NBC brought color to a growing proportion of its entertainment shows, while its parent company, RCA, built and promoted the sale of color television receivers, color became in 1966 a keenly competitive force in advertising. It swept across the program schedule like a tidal wave, engulfing, along with everything else, television news. By 1967 there were color sets in 9,510,000 homes, and sales continued to show an upward curve. In the live form, in fact in all forms of electronic journalism, formerly black and white tools of the trade—television cameras, film, and tape—were colorized so that news from the scene and from the studio achieved the same look of reality as that of the beautifully mounted shows concerned with nonreality. Both network and station news have gone to color, and although a number of stations have lagged behind the pack, news in color is in their plans and not far away.

The live television form discussed in this chapter is largely an instrument of the networks, and—except for sports—not of the local stations over which these programs are seen. Covering massive and often multilocational events—especially when they consume considerable air time—is a very expensive proposition, beyond the means of the average station. Aside from sports, most stations produce very little in the live, remote category. They settle for filming or video taping, and present condensed versions of the event as specials or on news programs. A striking exception to this rule is the all-out live contribution made by local stations in emergencies. This service needs attention all its own, and will get it when we discuss the station in its community.

Luckily for the country, the networks invest the money, time, and effort necessary to give us live coverage of significant events, even though they can rarely recover their financial investment. Frank Stanton, President of CBS, Inc., announced recently that the cost to CBS for four days of televised congressional hearings was just under one million dollars, to which must be added the loss in commercial revenue—over one million dollars—on canceled programs for the five stations CBS owns. It is reported that the day-long coverage of Pope Paul's visit cost the three networks $10,000,000 in revenues.

But this kind of coverage makes a vital contribution to the public good, and the size of its audiences and the appreciation some of them bother to express show how worthwhile it is. For example, 47.7 million Americans are estimated to have watched the 1964 election returns, and 48.8 million tuned in on the Gemini Four (space walk) flight. The peak audience for the Pope's visit was said to be 70 million, and a total of 140 million are supposed to have tuned in at some time during that day.

Live coverage does more than eliminate delay in reporting the story to people. By commanding airtime many times the length of other news programs, it permits a continuing, uncut version of the story to unfold before the viewer as in effect an antidote to a highly condensed form which is most often the mark of broadcast journalism. And there is no doubt that live television adds to the tendency of people to look upon television as their most important source of news and to accord it loyalty and trust.

FOUR

THE
DAILY NEWS
PROGRAM

While a live television event commands as much airtime as the length and import of the story dictate, almost the opposite is true of the regularly scheduled news program. The day-to-day routine of the television newsman is circumscribed by the basic restrictions of time and the necessity for condensation of material. In comparing the broadcast with the daily newspaper, one must remember that the word content of a half-hour news program is less than that of a single page of the *New York Times*. So, the electronic newsman can present only a capsule of the total product of his newspaper brethren. Further, in half an hour a newspaper reader can absorb many more words than an announcer can speak. The reader can choose from among more stories. He can go into detail on individual stories. And he can choose freely to concentrate on those stories that interest him most.

As a listener and viewer, the same individual loses his freedom to choose, and he must accept the newscaster's selection. These differences between printed and broadcast news are basic to an understanding of the nature of the regularly scheduled news program. The newsman— dependent on limited time instead of stretchable space— has to think about the limits of his audience's attention span. He must select the news items that will interest the most people, knowing that he has not the time to be all things to all men. He must judiciously make use of feature items—not front page news—that will help hold his audience with a change of pace.

When he is through he will still not have satisfied everyone, and he will not have supplied as much news as other media—newspapers, news magazines, opinion magazines, and the like. For radio and television cannot provide in their daily news programs all that is required to keep the American public well informed. Responsible members of the broadcast news fraternity make no such claim. On the contrary, their audiences are encouraged by broadcasters of the Walter Cronkite-David Brinkley stripe to supplement radio and television news with adequate reading of printed news. This, in order to avoid the superficial judgments that would otherwise grow out of complete dependence on the condensed offerings of broadcasting.

With the special requirements placed on it as a headline service, and by virtue of its need to be clear and accurate under the handicap of brevity, broadcasting has felt the need for the widest spread of sources for its news. It draws its voice-only reports, its film, live, and tape audio-visual reports, on-the-spot, remote, and communications satellite pickups, not only from its own reporters and correspondents but from such diversified sources as police radio bands and a part-time stringer in Afghanistan. The broadcast newsroom makes use of local, regional, national, and international wire services, of its own regular staffers, of its special beat reporters and its bureaus in major cities here and overseas. It depends on exchange arrangements with broadcasting organizations in other parts of the region, the country, or the world; on stories dug up by enterprise and investigative reporters; and on its own carefully kept "futures" file, which gives it a flagging system for stories that can be known about in advance.

In recent years, greater insistence on leaving nothing to chance has brought increased use of the broadcast newsman with his own, first-hand, on-the-spot reporting of a story, where possible directly from the scene of the news. Rapid improvement of equipment and techniques has made such coverage faster and easier than ever before. The highly organized team fielded today by network news establishments is geared to the day by day demands of the regular network news offerings, just as it is to the prolonged coverage of the live event. Judgments and critical selections that shape the daily news broadcast begin at the very top of the news organization, with the news executives of the network. Reporting to them are the editors or producers of programs. The latter command a corps of reporters, writers, cameramen, tape and film editors, technicians, and airmen. Several hours before a program is to be broadcast, the editor makes his plans and assigns his forces on the basis of the news then available. He anticipates later developments and he reserves sufficient flexibility to cope with the new news that will undoubtedly occur in the interval before airtime.

Once the news ingredients—the budget—are determined, the news-gathering manpower and tools are deployed to their tasks. Stories within coaxial cable or microwave relay reach of the network headquarters are prepared by network correspondents in the area or by reporters at local affiliated stations, and mounted for transmission and recording ahead of program time or for live transmission on the air. Stories from farther away already on film— Vietnam for instance—must be directed by air transportation to points within reach for feeding into the show.

After the news has been gathered and late-breaking additions made, it must be processed, edited, boiled down to fit in the package that will eventually be on the air. To the written stories that will be read by newscasters are added the silent and sound film, video and audio tapes, still photographs, maps, and art work. The final script incorporates all the ingredients and becomes the master from which all program personnel works. At this point the team of directors and the studio and projection crews move in to back up the on-air communicators—the anchor men and on-air reporters. Their mission is to bring all to final fruition and present as crisp, effective, and professional a news program as possible.

Network news organizations have been called upon to deliver their major daily news package in a new size in the last few years, as a result of executive decisions to increase manpower and budget and to double the newstime. NBC led the way in 1963 by expanding its Huntley-Brinkley Report from fifteen minutes to half an hour. CBS soon did the same with The Evening News with Walter Cronkite. By early 1967 Peter Jennings' time was doubled by ABC.

The jump from fifteen to thirty minutes by NBC and CBS for their prestigious evening news shows sparked a key upward turn in the whole television regular news program field. Since 1963, the network news programs have been lengthened and new ones have been added— notably in the previously neglected weekend period. Total air minutes of news available nationally each week is now, in 1967, three times what it was five years ago.

To meet the added challenge produced by the expansion of scheduled news and in a general across-the-board effort to upgrade all of its products, the network organization has mustered its most massive combination yet of men and materials. NBC lists a worldwide staff of 900 men and women; CBS claims 800; ABC, 750. These are full-time people. Also available are numerous "stringers" and local affiliated station reporters who are called on when there is news of national interest in their area. NBC News estimates an annual expenditure of $70 million on news; CBS, $50 million; and ABC, $40 million. On any day it is a pretty good bet that a total of 150 people are involved one way or another in the production of the Huntley-Brinkley or the Cronkite program.

To what purpose, the toil of such armies of electronic men? What is the caliber of their news product and what effect do they have on the television audience? With the explosion of 1963 it could be expected, first of all, that longer news programs meant more news or more thorough treatment of stories. In the area called hard news, spot or breaking news of most significance to most people, both these things have happened. It is with hard news that the network weekday evening news (and other network news shows too) are filled, with small remaining percentages— other than commercial time—given over to features, sports, humor, and background pieces, and in some cases special interpretive segments.

The hard news concentrates on stories of national and international significance. Politics, government, foreign affairs, and in these days of course the Vietnam war, are the categories of news treated daily. In a good many cities, network viewers are exposed to more hard news from Washington and worldwide than they can get from their local newspapers. Another kind of hard news—the tabloid story of highway crash, violent crime, and gore—is nearly nonexistent unless the story is on a scale which cannot be ignored.

The background, non-deadline piece, sometimes running to three or four minutes, provides viewers with background on a political or social issue, a scientific discovery, an educational or cultural subject. This story form, running two or three times the length of the average deadline story, could never find room on the five- or rarely on the fifteen-minute versions of television news. As the volume of hard news on a particular day permits, the short feature or even shorter humorous story gets an airing as a change of pace and mood from the usually heavy nature of the news of the day.

The networks are still equivocal about the inclusion of commentary on the news program. As of now, Howard K. Smith on the Peter Jennings show and Eric Sevareid on CBS are the only ones. They are not billed as such, and they occupy a quite minor percentage of airtime, not necessarily on a nightly basis. Commentary and news analysis are a special form of electronic journalism about which there is still disagreement even as to their definition; the question will get some attention later on.

The network's number one news programs reach nearly every corner of the country each week night. Approximately 200 stations carry Huntley-Brinkley and the same number broadcast Walter Cronkite, while 160 carry Peter Jennings. NBC rates its nightly audience at 18,540,000. CBS has Cronkite with 16,730,000, and ABC estimates its show draws 7,580,000. Tens of thousands of persons in the United States see the same program and share a common experience. Just as with the live, special event, it is this commonality of viewer experience which gives special meaning to the national impact of television news. The ramifications of the mass viewing of a Morley Safer battle story from Vietnam on CBS or a series of civil rights marches and demonstrations on NBC can't be delineated or measured exactly, but those responsible at the network news establishments are never free of the sobering thought that their "instant national newspaper" reaches into the minds of a whole people.

If millions of Americans watch television network news, millions also watch the news programs produced in their own cities by their own television stations. And what the better local stations have done to strengthen their news product is proportionally at least as impressive as what the networks have done. Some of this growth came as a chain reaction from the network news expansion of 1963–64. NBC and CBS not only set an example; they created a scheduling problem for their affiliated stations. The quarter hour of local news adjacent to the network news which worked fine when the total came to half an hour, didn't work as well when the total came to the odd length of 45 minutes. In many cities quarter-hour shows soon became half-hour shows. Some news-minded stations moved up to a full hour of their own news. Ten and eleven p.m. local news doubled in length, and local news found its place on Saturdays and Sundays to a greater degree than ever before. Independent television stations felt the competition, and many of them followed the pattern of the affiliates.

In a period of a few years, good stations in larger-size

cities have boosted their weekly hours of news programming from the four-and-a-half to seven range to the ten to fourteen range. Instead of settling for two or three newscasts a day on weekdays and perhaps one each on Saturday and Sunday, stations went to five, six, or seven news segments each weekday and five or six on weekends. Budgets were raised to new heights; many of them doubled in a short time, and in the large cities, station news department budgets of $750,000 and more are a fact of life. NBC recently announced a two-million-dollar annual budget for its West Coast news operation at Los Angeles's KNBC. More money has enabled news directors to build bigger staffs. WDSU, New Orleans (43rd in market size) has sixteen people in news. There are thirty at WTVJ, Miami, the 24th market; 46 at KSTP, Minneapolis-St. Paul; 72 at KNXT, Los Angeles, and 145 at WCBS, New York.

At these stations one or two anchor men broadcast from the news studio in basically the same way as in network news. But in the current larger-budget, larger-staff situation, these men are backed up by reporters who cover the local and regional stories first hand. The audience gets (via film or tape, and occasionally live) the on-the-spot account which is so important to the accuracy and the excitement of the television story presentation. An increasing number of these local reporters are assigned special beats, a long-time practice of daily newspapers, which gives them a chance to gain expertise in a particular news area, with consequent improvement in their reporting and benefit to the viewers. In Chicago, Minneapolis, and New Orleans—just to name three—there are television political beat reporters who cover state, county, and municipal government. WFBM, Indianapolis, even has a special reporter in the field of education. News Director Bob

Gamble says: "After all, the schools have the biggest budget in town and get more of the taxpayers' money." Stations further broaden their news gathering and filmed coverage through stringers, part-time men on call in areas not quickly accessible to the home staff. They are frequently equipped with cameras to treat the story television's way. WOOD-TV, Grand Rapids, Michigan, covers large parts of its big state with such men; and Jim Byron, WBAP, Fort Worth, has stringers "all over Texas."

Film and videotape occupy a larger role in local news presentation. KCRA, Sacramento, California, shoots 60,000 feet a month in film alone. Sioux City, Iowa (Station KTIV), accounts for 17,000 a month; KRON, in San Francisco, ticks off 75,000; WCBS-TV, New York, 125,000. (125,000 feet translates into nearly 60 hours' worth of film, which in turn averages out to two hours' worth of newsfilm shot every day.)

The kind of stories the station news team puts on its air, as one would expect, runs heavily to local news, leaving the national and world news to the networks with which the stations are affiliated. The independent station naturally must find other sources for its Washington and international coverage. But the backbone of television station news is news of the area and of the community. Within that compass lies a whole range of news that can be covered. It can't all be covered, so what stories? What kind of news? Veteran station News Director Bill McGivern, KSTP, St. Paul, agrees with David Brinkley, who said, "News is what I say it is." But Mr. McGivern thinks the television newsman has the obligation to pick the most substantial and important stories in his region.

Many stations used to, and some still do, let pictorial values govern what goes on the news program. A lot of trivia cluttered up so-called news shows as a result. Worse yet, many a station concentrated its news on fatal accidents, crimes of violence, and lurid stories in what was really the cheapest kind of tabloid newscast. The trend in journalism is now away from both of these bad habits, and in television at least not many of the die-hards remain. News director Travis Linn (WFAA, Dallas) says his programs are getting away from crime and violence. Dick Eardley in Boise says he has been able to train his audience away from tabloid stories. "Crime news," says Lamar Crosby (KID, Idaho Falls) "is not a community contribution." Jon Poston (KTIV, Sioux City) says that his audience ratings prove that the abandonment of tabloid news was a wise move.

The content of a one-hour local evening news program monitored at random on WCBS-TV New York early in 1967 showed this allocation of time to different categories of news: New York City, 37 percent; regional, 14 percent; Washington and national, 10 percent; world, 9 percent. The remaining 30 percent included a science piece, the stock market, sports, and weather. There were no stories of sensational, tabloid character.

One of the big community contributions of television is covering the news of civic affairs—city, county, and state. These visually static stories are getting airtime, and are being dealt with by more knowledgeable television newsmen than was the case only a few years ago. Some stations go beyond this. KMTV, Omaha, has its own specialist in foreign affairs, John Labochek, a long-time foreign correspondent who has a three-minute spot on the nightly news and who travels abroad to keep up with what's going on, shooting film en route as the base for documentaries which he airs on the station when he returns.

The quality of the news varies, of course, from station to station and from market to market. A two-station market in one city may boast two good news operations; in another, not even one. The same is true in three-station and in multi-station cities. In some markets competition between stations is as hot as that among the networks. Chicago seems currently to be the best example of this, with four stations fighting it out hammer and tongs.

Network and station news competition has brought about in many cities a scheduling strategy worthy of the most wily entrepreneurs on Madison Avenue. If your news is strong enough, you meet the competition head to head by scheduling your news at the same time he does. If you can't buck him, you air at another time. A station may decide to place its own evening news ahead of its network news or vice versa. In 1965, local news on KNXT was so strong in southern California that NBC threw its first string—Huntley and Brinkley—against the CBS station's local news program to improve its competitive position. In Atlanta, the combination of Huntley-Brinkley and the crack local news operation of WSB so overshadowed the CBS outlet that it did not carry the Cronkite news show at all. Network flagship stations WNBC-TV and WCBS-TV in New York battle for the six to seven o'clock audience to try to pass along an edge to their network news programs at seven. Rather than be caught in this murderous cross-fire, WABC-TV starts its local news at five.

The television news program is no better than its direct link with the viewer; this link is the on-the-air communicator. Whether or not it is good for the air person to become a star, for a show-business aspect to be injected into electronic news, for a personality to become a part of the news that is delivered—these are nevertheless the realities. As the big network news names are famous across the land, their counterparts on local stations are celebrated in their communities. Ralph Renick (WTVJ) is as well known in Miami, as is Walter Cronkite nationally. Len O'Connor has been a fixture for years on NBC in Chicago. Before television ever started, Cedric Adams put WCCO, Minneapolis, on the map.

This star system, created by the public, is not likely to change either at the national or the local level. What is changing and will continue to change is the caliber and capability of the star. Up to now, too many electronic communicators with a knack for holding an audience have been "readers"—personalities with no news credentials. Now emerging is the combination of sound newsman-good communicator, and he is worth special attention in another chapter of this book.

News programs have always held interest for radio and television audiences, but the leap forward these last few years in television news has been matched by a marked upswing in viewership. Whether there was a latent audience demand that the expanded news met or whether expanded news, once available, stimulated new viewer interest or both—the fact is that more viewers are making a habit of watching more television news. The Nielson audience-rating service shows that between 1962 and 1965 the homes using television in the period from 6:30 to 7:30 P.M.—which is reserved almost exclusively for news—went from 46.4 to 56.2, five viewers where only four watched at the earlier date. According to the same source, the total national audience for the three big networks' evening news shows rose by one million viewers from March, 1964, to March, 1965. At the station level, the late news (11 P.M. in some time zones, 10 P.M. in others) shows the same kind

42

of audience growth. This time period remains the stronghold of local news. Watching it becomes the last thing before bed in millions of American homes.

Some of this audience is motivated by this additional viewing to follow up what it sees by reading newspapers' and news magazines' more detailed stories and analysis, just as the sports fan is apt to do after watching the game on television. Some are lulled by the longer stint in front of the screen into feeling they have all the news without reading. But either way, as Roper found in his survey, there is a higher degree of acceptance now than ever before of what television news says, and a tendency to rate it as the primary news source among all the media.

This chapter would not be complete without a reference to radio's role in regularly scheduled news broadcasting. Radio continues to enjoy an edge in speed and flexibility over television. Its economics make possible more news programs and a much higher proportion of total schedule devoted to news. Radio is more readily receivable by more people. The transistor audience and the audience on wheels, for instance, are radio audiences.

In the live event category, television ranks well ahead of radio where a choice is available to the audience. With documentaries and other programs in depth, television replaced radio to the point where such programs nearly disappeared from the sound medium, although in the mid-sixties there is some revival of news-in-depth radio, including a real move toward the "talk" station. Radio, on the other hand, has very much held its own in two areas: the frequent, recurring news program, and the disaster or emergency service. The latter will be discussed in a later chapter.

A 1966 Trendex survey shows that during two-thirds

of the daytime—except in fact for the 6 P.M. to midnight time—radio is dominant over television as a spot news source. The brief round-up of the latest news every half hour or every hour makes it easy for people at home, at work, in cars, and on holiday to get the gist of what's going on, or as Eric Sevareid, referring to the extreme brevity of such newscasts, puts it, "To find out what *hasn't* happened."

In four cities as this is written, listeners do not have to wait even a few minutes for news on radio. Chicago, Philadelphia, Washington, and New York each has a station which programs news twenty-four hours a day. WINS, the Westinghouse station in New York, airs its news on a thirty-minute headway, so that each thirty minutes, day and night, a listener gets a new start, but he can come in at any time and within thirty minutes get the full round-up. Two of these all-news stations are now operating in the black, so it would seem that in areas of population concentration, at least, this form of special news service will be permanently available.

FIVE

IN–DEPTH
PROGRAMS

The live, special-event form of television journalism treats a story as it unfolds at the pace or at approximately the pace of the story itself. The regular news program treats many stories in highly condensed form. In terms of ground covered, the programs called here "in-depth" programs fall somewhere in between these two. In this form, a half hour or longer is devoted to the examination of one story or one subject and is designed to provide background or analysis. It attempts to explore, to give perspective, to bring the viewer a better understanding of a situation, a subject, or an issue, of which only the surface is touched by the daily news.

I include various kinds of television formats when referring to in-depth programming: the documentary, the "news special" against a deadline, the depth interview, the panel discussion. These may be regularly scheduled on a weekly or monthly basis or they may be dropped in —pre-empting a scheduled program—as timeliness or other factors dictate. Both network and station news and public affairs departments make frequent use of one or another of these formats, and recently they have run such a gamut of subject matter that it takes the broadest definition of journalism to hold them all.

On the average, in-depth programs do not command anything like the audience for news and for live programs. Those who do watch can be moved, stimulated, informed, and educated by well conceived, intelligent broadcasts of this type. Though some of the formats discussed in the following pages do not make use of television's best attributes, the impact is still a telling one, and even some non-readers will submit to in-depth programming, if their attention is caught.

The major news story which breaks suddenly or undergoes a new turn, or an important story continually in the news, prompt the topical special. This may be a single program—to look into the meaning behind a Harlem riot or the reasons back of an unexpected legislative action on a tax bill. Or it may be a regular weekly program to provide a continuing examination of a story like the war in Vietnam.

Regardless of the form of the program, it is distinct from other in-depth treatments because it is prepared in a limited time. A television news team which is experienced and doesn't have to worry too much about budgets can put together a news special in short order. This may cost it the perspective that more time would permit, but it does give the audience additional dimension to the story while it is still fresh. Here is the chronology of the development of one—or rather two—network news specials.

The big news on Sunday, July 31, 1966, was the rejection by the machinists union of a White House-endorsed settlement of a 24-day strike against five major U. S. airlines. About noon the next day, CBS News officials decided to produce a special hour on the strike story for broadcast Tuesday night at 10:00. At the moment this decision was being made, a demented student named Charles Whitman went on a shooting rampage on the campus of the University of Texas, the outcome of which was death for fifteen people including Whitman himself. This was to mean—although the CBS men did not know it then—that the news department would be involved in the production of two fast-deadline news specials at the same time.

For the special on the airlines strike, producer Les Midgley assembled his fifteen-man news team very early Monday afternoon, outlined plans for the hour-long show, and dispatched them to their appointed tasks. In New York the job began of selecting, screening, and editing news film and videotape of the 25-day television news coverage of the strike story. The CBS Washington Bureau got the job of lining up interviews with relevant spokesmen: William J. Curtin, principal negotiator for the airlines; P. L. Siemiller, President of the union; union members who voted for rejection of the settlement; Senator Wayne Morse, who had headed President Johnson's committee which earlier had recommended a solution to the dispute; and Secretary of Labor W. Willard Wirtz.

New York writers began marshaling the information and factual material necessary to fill out the picture story for the program. The writing of the show began on Monday, was not finished until late Tuesday, the broadcast day. The writing, needed to tie in the new interviews and statements, was assigned to the Washington staff. Walter Cronkite was cleared for anchor man duties; a total of four Washington correspondents participated in the filming and taping of interviews.

Just after 7:30 P.M. on Monday—while the strike special was beginning to take form—came the decision to do a crash, half-hour special on the Texas massacre. Cronkite's Evening News had just aired the story nationally, and everything pointed to an in-depth version as added elements turned up. The time of 11:30—less than four hours away—was selected as airtime, and CBS stations across the country were immediately alerted, since that hour is one during which stations normally do local programming.

Midgley, his regular staff tied up with the strike special, had to round up additional manpower—writers, film editors, a director, and studio crew—for the new assignments. He reached Walter Cronkite, whose work seems never done, and put him on the anchor job. Carl Bakal, author of a new book on a pertinent subject—*The Right to Bear Arms*—was located and persuaded to appear on the program. In the meantime, the CBS crew in Austin, who had covered the Whitman story for the *Evening News*, was put back to work.

CBS correspondent David Schoumacher and his camera team were asked to find new material to supplement what New York had received from them earlier, and 10:30 was set as the time for them to feed it so it could be taped in New York for incorporation into the air show. Technical difficulties ensued, and it was 11:25 before the last of the Austin part of the story reached headquarters. With a rough spot here and there, the sniper special got on the air and concluded with a thoughtful and thought-provoking interview of author Bakal, by Cronkite.

Producer Midgley had little time to relax; for him it was back to the airline strike program, now less than 24 hours away. By the middle of Tuesday, the broad outline of the show had been generally determined. However, it was to undergo changes until the last moment. Facts were collected, writing was progressing, and interviews were taped or scheduled. The Washington Bureau had a new angle—a statement from an official of an electrician's union that if the machinists' settlement should exceed the President's non-inflationary guidelines, then all bets were off for adherence by other unions. Washington reported that they could not promise to deliver Willard Wirtz; it would be late if at all. Midgley decided to insert the Washington portion of the hour by means of a switch and a direct, live feed during the broadcast instead of trying to preassemble all the ingredients in New York.

Evaluation of the content of spokesmen's statements already recorded prompted the production team to allocate the most airtime to Curtin and to Siemiller. Others were edited down to shorter time segments. Senator Wayne Morse and the electrician's spokesman were scheduled, and a hole saved for the Labor Secretary, which was finally filled; his statement was taped in the Washington studio at 5:30 P.M.

Only now, a few hours before deadline, was it possible to turn out a final line-up sheet, detailing all show segments in their order and the time allotted to each. Editing and final writing went on almost to airtime. Cronkite himself wrote the two-minute summation for the close of the show. At ten o'clock CBS viewers saw a three-and-a-half-minute introduction depicting the impact on the country of 26 days of interrupted commercial airline service, and "The Airline Strike: What Price Settlement?" was on the air.

How was it possible to bring off two such programs on such short notice? Newsman Midgley says the basic reason is that everyone on the team knew what to do.

A continuing story, as distinct from a spot story like the strike or the sniper in Austin, can and does get constant attention—Vietnam, for instance. As the size of the Vietnam story and our preoccupation with it increased, the news coverage and actualities were backed up with frequent special programs by the networks. Although many of these were pegged to happenings in the news, the allotting of larger amounts of time made it possible to do more than an instant review or analysis and to turn to a number of facets of our complicated Far Eastern commitment and deal with them in some depth. As Frank Stanton, President of CBS, put it:

. . . because no war is fought in a military vacuum, we have tried to show its social, economic and political context, the melancholy plight of the noncombatants, the efforts to repair the homes and restore the lives of civilian victims of the Vietcong, and the long, slow, laborious plantings of the seeds of social progress, economic reform, and environmental improvements. And we have tried also to report both support and dissent of our public policy, not to persuade, but to stimulate thought and to provoke discussion.[1]

During the first half of 1966, CBS aired one CBS Reports program on the subject of Vietnam and sixteen other programs in the category of "news special" alone. NBC in the same period logged nearly fifty-five hours of specials, presidential addresses, Pentagon news briefings, and hearings of the Senate Foreign Relations Committee. In April, 1966, NBC inaugurated a Sunday weekly review on Vietnam.

The undated documentary, such as those in the NBC White Paper series, the CBS Reports, and the ABC Scope, treats a subject not tied to breaking news or one which will not lose its effectiveness if its broadcast time is months away from its inception. Here, of course, the producers can have more of everything than they can with deadline specials. There is room for expanded planning, additional research time, greater refining, and increased time for a mature point of view. This application of news and of production skills is exemplified in documentaries of the sixties like Harvest of Shame (CBS), Red China (NBC), Walking Hard (about juvenile delinquency) (ABC), the Water Famine, The Pope and the Vatican, Cigarettes—A Collision of Interests, and Walk in My Shoes (an ABC stunner about the lot of the Negro). Obviously, they range widely in their subjects.

But in the last few years there has been an additional broadening of the scope of documentaries, by which the news tent stretches over many subjects not ordinarily thought of as news. Some include history, literature, music, art, and the personal profile or biography. Even the foibles of our society have become more prominent. For example, programs like the Saga of Western Man series, the Kremlin, the Louvre, the World of Jacqueline Kennedy, Robert Frost—American Poet, Pablo Casals, the Great American Funeral are gaining more widespread attention. And contemporary documentarians find popular topics in the fields of nature, travel, and sports, too.

Some subjects are excitingly visual and make natural documentaries. The adaptation from Theodore White's book, *The Making of the President*, with miles of film and tape to draw on, was one of these. Then there are subjects unsympathetic to the television form, such as the two-part CBS Reports series on the U. S. Supreme Court, not made easier by the traditional ban on cameras at court sessions. A remarkable pair of programs emerged. And it is a sign of the maturing of television news that it is no longer frightened away from treating an unvisual story if the story is important.

The documentary has lately broken out of its half-hour and hour pattern. In three notable instances there have been entire prime-time evenings devoted to one documentary. NBC pioneered with a three-hour study of the Negro in America in 1964. In September, 1965, the same network devoted the whole evening to Our Foreign Policy, and a year later presented a major three-and-a-half-hour documentary on crime in the United States. ABC produced a four-hour program on Africa, for broadcast in September, 1967.

Brief documentary background pieces have been finding their way into the body of the expanded network and local station news programs. Running three, four, or five minutes, these consist of capsulized versions of in-depth treatments, which sounds like a contradiction in terms. But whatever they may lose in the condensation, their advocates point out they gain a considerably larger audience than they would as full-length programs of their own. If the story is worth it, it may be treated in three- to five-minute segments over a period of days within the news program. This has the advantage of coming back to a topic again and again instead of treating it only once.

Both networks and television stations offer, in addition to ad hoc specials and documentaries produced over longer periods, "talk" programs which go into more depth on news and on issues than is possible on the daily news. One variety is represented by Meet the Press and its counterparts on other networks. The same format appears in local station versions all across the country.

Depth interviews, panels of experts, debates between political candidates or government officials are other ways in which television journalism puts meat on the bones of the news. Still another is taking the television camera to a scheduled event like the town meeting, public gathering, the campus symposium, the teach-in. As mentioned earlier, CBS even goes beyond our borders with what it calls The Town Meeting of the World. The audience-pulling power of such public affairs programming—lacking the visual and actuality advantages of news and documentary—depends on how important the participants are and how controversial or how exciting the subject.

"Talk" programs are easier and cheaper to produce than documentaries or specials. At both local and national levels, there is keen competition to land the public figure-of-the-hour for your program, but public figures at every level see television as a valuable means of exposure, and there are enough to go round. Most receive no honorarium for appearing, and the behind-the-camera production team is comparatively small.

Cost is a different matter for any documentary that goes beyond a compilation of existing material. A rule of thumb is that the documentary cost runs to a minimum of a thousand dollars an air minute. It can run much higher than that, and may involve a number of film crews, much travel and location shooting, and the editing of ten to fifty times as much material as is seen on the final program, not to mention the high-priced brain power that goes into the inception, the planning, the research, and the writing. And that last is vital.

Veteran broadcast correspondent David Schoenbrun says of the documentary: "The result can never be any better than the good research and consistent reportorial care that goes into the job, and these things take time and professional competence." And they take the right combination of a good writer-reporter and an able producer, the man who knows how to use the sight-sound medium effectively to insure that serious material makes as attractive and clear an impact on an audience as does the more obviously telegenic material in entertainment. ABC correspondent Howard K. Smith describes it as combining integrity with great reporting, writing, and showmanship. Showmanship is no longer a nasty word in this field. The best producers, the best writers, the best on-air talent in television journalism today demonstrate when they broadcast that in television, effectiveness equates with showmanship and that integrity does not have to suffer.

How such programs are born and how they are produced can be better understood by two case histories, both admittedly rather out-of-the-ordinary and very successful efforts in the documentary form—NBC's The Tunnel (1962) and CBS's Biography of a Bookie Joint (1961).

In May of 1962, NBC Berlin correspondent Piers Anderton had a visit from three West German engineering students, who revealed that they were digging a tunnel under the Wall to help a group of East Germans escape and would sell NBC the film rights for $20,000. Back in New York, Producer Reuven Frank saw a means of dramatically conveying to Americans the deep desire for freedom in the captive Communist countries, and when the authenticity of the project and the good faith of the engineers had been established he approved the deal—for $12,500.

A plan was worked out to coordinate NBC's filming with the subterranean labors, and then under the greatest of difficulties (aside from the obvious ones, the need for absolute secrecy, the additional one of shooting movie film in a dark, wet, and cramped tunnel where there was just space enough for the diggers and the earth removers), cameraman Peter Dehmel recorded the story yard by yard through the long summer. To complicate matters, another tunnel in which rival CBS was involved was put out of business upon being discovered by the East Germans before it was completed. The U. S. State Department looked into the affair and then put strong pressure on NBC to abandon its project. NBC kept on, and the tunnel was completed on September 14th and became the avenue of escape for 59 refugees—the largest number since the Wall was erected. Dehmel got the most dramatic footage of all, of course, the actual escape through the tunnel.

When NBC announced the televising of the documentary, the State Department moved in again to try to stop it on the grounds that families left behind in East Germany might be endangered. NBC was able to demonstrate to officials in West Berlin that all identities had been carefully concealed; the Berlin Senate gave its opinion that showing the film would be in the interest of Berlin; and in November the United States public saw what Robert Kintner considers "one of the great achievements of broadcasting journalism."

If The Tunnel was a clandestine affair, so was the Biography of a Bookie Joint. Executive Producer Fred Friendly had long wanted to bring before the public the moral issue of illegal gambling that goes on in many parts of the country. In the spring of 1961, he assigned producer-writer Jay McMullen to do the story on the bookmaking business in Boston, as an example of what was going on nationally. McMullen found a key-maker's shop which was openly conducting a bookie business with no interference from the police. He rented a second-floor flat across the street, slipped his camera and crew inside, and went into the documentary business. Over a period of weeks of shooting, he accumulated a web of visual evidence of what was going on. He even got some film of bets being taken inside the shop by concealing a miniature camera in a lunch box he carried into the place.

During and after the filming episode, the CBS team went through a painstaking period of research, fact digging, and fact checking. They were playing with dynamite—Boston police officers were seen in the film footage entering and leaving the bookie joint—and for legal as well as ethical reasons they had to be sure their story was accurate in every detail. Thousands of feet of film were edited with care, filmed interviews with appropriate spokesmen were inserted, the script written and gone over again and again. Biography went on the air on November 30, 1961, and in Boston the cries of anguish and of outrage didn't die down for months. But as Friendly had hoped, the effect was national. Documentary scholar A. William Bluem says: ". . . this single program created far greater impact than many more sensational treatments of similar topics."[2]

At the station level, naturally, everything is on a smaller scale as to budget, production manpower, and facilities, precluding ambitious endeavors like those just described. Stations generally confine their documentary efforts to local issues or stories that lie within their capacities. And most of them turn out a considerably smaller volume of costly programs and more of the simple, talk-type show. However, a 1965 survey is encouraging on this score. It showed that among stations with active news operations, nearly half produced a documentary each month; a tenth produced one more often than that; a tenth produced from six to nine documentaries a year; and the rest produced one occasionally or are just beginning to get into the documentary form. Market size is not necessarily a factor. As might be expected, there are stations in New York, Chicago, and San Francisco turning out one a week. But WBT, Charlotte, North Carolina (the thirtieth market in the country in point of size) produced sixteen in twelve months; WDSU, New Orleans (the 46th market) produced one a month; so did KID-TV, a station in a wide place in the road called Idaho Falls.

For most stations the instant news special poses prohibitive problems and is usually confined to those in large markets. Even they have to stretch, as the following case history shows.

Early in the evening on Sunday, January 31, 1965, Fred Christiansen left his home in Chicago's West Side and walked down the street to get a pack of cigarettes. As he came to a corner, three young men jumped out of a car parked there and attacked him. One carried a 22-caliber rifle and shot Christiansen several times. Another tore off his wrist watch and grabbed his wallet containing ten dollars. Then they drove off. Eyewitnesses said the attackers seemed to be laughing. When they got to Christiansen, he was dying.

Around 4:00 A.M. the following Wednesday, the early morning news staff at ABC's Chicago station, WBKB, got the flash that police had arrested three teen-age suspects in the Christiansen murder. They dispatched a film crew. Shortly afterward, police established that the accused slayers were goofball addicts—in fact were high on pep pills at the time of the murder. By 8:00 A.M. WBKB's newsmen were discussing a news special to be broadcast later the same day. It made sense. They had good film footage shot that morning of the three suspects shortly after their capture as well as film shot earlier at the time of the killing. It was an especially shocking crime, and moreover, the police findings rekindled the controversy involving traffic in pep pills and goofballs to teen-agers in Chicago, which made it an issue worth special attention.

A thirty-minute program was decided on, to be aired just ahead of the station's 6 P.M. evening news. News Director Dick Goldberg defined the task: "We had approximately nine hours to prepare an instant special dealing with the actual killing and its attendant shock waves; the quick and efficient police work in tracking down the killers; background information on the suspects including the reason why they would kill a stranger for petty cash, and some examination of the illegal pep pill traffic in Chicago."

A station is not staffed like a network. Goldberg had to make heavy inroads on the staff normally responsible for the regular evening news show. Three of the four reporter-film camera teams he could muster were put on the pill story, leaving one to cover everything else in town. The first was assigned to cover the police angle, the second the backgrounds of the teen-age suspects, the third the pep pill part of the story.

By 2 P.M. nearly four thousand feet of film had been shot and was arriving in the newsroom. It included interviews with the Chicago Police Superintendent and a youth officer who had known the suspects previously, an interview with the mother of one boy and a letter written by another urging her son to accept whatever punishment he had coming, and a letter which revealed that the youngster was overprotected as a child, then permitted to come and go as he pleased when he reached his teens. WBKB's reporter established that two of the boys were from broken homes, victims of parental neglect. The reporter on the pill angle produced an interview with an official of the Federal Drug Administration on the effects of such pills on the nervous system and the problems the authorities were having in keeping them out of the hands of teen-agers.

News Director Goldberg and anchorman Frank Reynolds pitched in to help their news writers and film editors to refine over two hour's worth of material into a hard-core half hour under the pressures of a heartless clock. Anybody who paused a moment found himself working as frantically on the other—the regular—news show which could not be allowed to suffer, special or no special. And the job was made more demanding because the special would be stealing away the day's big story from the regular news.

Goldberg explained: "We completed the Pep Pill show at 5:20, a half-hour film package ready for air. Narration by Frank Reynolds and all super cards to be live from our news studio. No time for rehearsal or run through; the Director used the remaining ten minutes to mark his script." Pills of Death had its half hour on the air, and except for a couple of words lost on the sound track, the program was flawless. At the end, Reynolds laid down his special script, picked up his news script, launched into the Six O'Clock Report, and told Chicagoans what else happened in Chicago that day.

Educational (noncommercial) television has dealt itself a hand in the in-depth field. As in commercial television this has happened at the station level, as well as in the programming of the National Educational Television (NET) network. NET is a program producer and distributor via film and tape to its member educational television stations. There are 116 such stations in forty-one states, including the District of Columbia and Puerto Rico—so there is potential here. In the area of public affairs programming, educational television enjoys one great advantage and labors under another great disadvantage. It can and does air such programs in prime viewing time; but it has less money to spend than anybody else. Until the budgets are better, this arm of television cannot consistently deliver in its top air time the equal of what commercial television produces and then sometimes relegates to marginal broadcast time.

But educational television gets A for effort, and it has turned out first-rate programs, some of which show a candor and courage about tough subjects that are rare or missing in the commercial record. There is never likely to be on commercial air a series like NET's which evaluates for the consumer the worth or worthlessness of different products of American industry being sold to the public. And though there is plenty of private griping in television newsrooms about government management of news, it was on educational television in the summer of 1966 that four American correspondents sharply and publicly criticized Defense Department information policies and press briefings in regard to Vietnam with such comments as: Arthur Sylvester, Assistant Secretary of Defense for Public Affairs was "one of the great practitioners of the art of news management," and that the Administration and "particularly Secretary of Defense McNamara have deliberately misled American public opinion."

The in-depth program is or can be an arm of electronic journalism that is of deepest importance. It can do more than inform, it can enlighten its audience. It can get at the essence of a thousand questions that affect our lives. Whether or how well it enlightens its audience will come under discussion at some length in later chapters.

SIX

THE
EDITORIAL

The editorial as discussed in this chapter is the news form in which the point of view expressed is not that of an individual journalist but that of the broadcasting organization itself. The subject may range from the man-eating shark to the endorsement of a candidate for political office. The editorial may come as the concluding portion of a documentary program, within the body of a hard news program, or just prior to the switch to the ball park for the Major League game. In any case, it will be identified as an editorial expression of the management.

The labeled editorial is a broadcast *station* phenomenon. Instances at the national network level are few, and at this time none of the networks shows signs of assuming the editorial as a regular responsibility. The networks rationalize this by saying that to editorialize would be to speak through the transmitters of hundreds of affiliated stations whose owners might not hold the same editorial view and to communities whose traditions, attitudes and problems vary too greatly on many subjects to allow the common application of one point of view. These are the very things which make the individual stations the natural place for editorials, and that is where they are found.

This form of journalism, the equivalent of the newspaper editorial page, arrived on the radio and television scene comparatively recently. In the early days of the Federal Communications Commission (FCC), the regulatory agency was inclined to the view that editorializing on the air was not the proper role of broadcasters. One station in Boston tried it and was taken to task in the historic Mayflower Case of 1941. Broadcasters took their cue, and editorials were left strictly to the print media even after the Commission reversed its position in 1949, specifically approving editorializing and establishing a set of ground rules. WMCA, an independent radio station in New York City, instituted regular editorials in 1954 and makes claim to being the first to do so. WTVJ, Miami, Florida, which makes a like claim for television, didn't begin until 1957. The 1960s arrived before any considerable number of stations engaged in the practice.

The recent growth has been phenomenal. According to a 1966 study conducted by the National Association of Broadcasters (NAB), more than 50 percent of radio and television stations do editorializing. Some deliver one a day, some weekly, some less often; some only when the spirit moves them on an issue they consider especially important. The rapid growth clearly indicates that editorials on the air are going to be a permanent and significant form of electronic journalism.

Since there are those who question whether broadcasters should take a point of view—as now condoned by the FCC—instead of confining their efforts to hard news, and live (actuality) and in-depth treatment of subjects and issues presented as objectively as possible, let's look at the thinking behind this form on the part of those who practice it.

The 1966 NAB survey showed that those stations which editorialize do so for one or more of the following reasons: to exert community responsibility and leadership; to enhance their reputations as reliable news media; to attract and build a larger audience; to comply with recommendations of the FCC or the NAB, and to reflect staff and management attitudes. Here is what some men say who are active in the field. News Director Don Mozley, KCBS, San Francisco (like WMCA, a pioneer): "A strong editorial policy is a testimony to a station's leadership. The station earns respect as its editorials earn respect." Dale Clark, Editorial Director of WAGA, Atlanta: "Our editorials get us involved in the community." Clayton Brace, Manager of KOGO, San Diego, decided his station should "deal itself a hand" in the power structure of the community. Manager Eldon Campbell of WFBM, Indianapolis, finds that editorializing gives broadcasters stature and "unique recognition . . . that at least you stand for something."

The air editorial is usually a one- to three-minute script read on microphone or camera by either the manager of the station or the news or editorial director. It is labeled as the opinion of the station or station management. Federal regulations require the script (the text) to be kept available for later inspection, and on-the-air rebuttal of the editorial is implicitly or explicitly invited by individuals, groups, or organizations holding another point of view. Many stations make large mailings of the editorial before or at the time it is put on the air, so that the text of what they are saying can be studied and agreed with or disagreed with.

The ideas for station editorial subjects, and decisions on what position the station will take, are cleared through an editorial board which usually includes executives of the station, an editorial director or writer, and the news director. As has been said, the frequency of editorials varies from station to station, but any given editorial usually receives from two to eight separate airings (more times on radio than on television) at different times in a day or two days, to reach different segments of the audience. Radio editorials may incorporate in the script with the reader's voice, the voices of officials or others whose statements are pertinent to the subject or documentary material. Television editorials may include appropriate visual material in the form of film, stills, maps, and charts. A strong editorializer, WDSU-TV, New Orleans, uses a daily cartoon to drive home its editorial point, and some other stations are beginning to adopt this telegenic technique.

Most editorializing stations concentrate on local and regional issues. Three things appear to account for their avoidance of national and international subjects. They are the editorialist's feeling that he has not sufficient knowledge or resources to deal with these subjects responsibly; and second, that they are less important for him to take time for than local questions. A third matter, at least with some, is that sharp division in the community may be produced by the editorial on national and world issues, or the reverse—that there's not enough public interest in such issues to justify them.

There are a multitude of local subjects, many of which reflect problems which are common to many communities of all sizes: criticism of local political leaders and local government; right to work laws; reapportionment; air and water pollution and fluoridation; housing and slums;

segregation; schools, antipoverty activity; traffic, parking, and freeways; crime; birth control; and taxes. Some stations make running campaigns of one or another of such local or regional issues. Some take up a subject only once, or they may return to it if they see no results from the first effort.

Frequently such editorials are calls for action, but not always. As the late Alan Newcomb, Public Affairs Director of WBTV, Charlotte, North Carolina, saw it, his editorials "should incite to thought rather than to action." Bruce Palmer of Oklahoma City says he has tried to bring about a "pattern of thinking, not just action in the community." At WOOD, Grand Rapids, the conviction is that there is nothing the station can do of greater value in the long run than to say: "We think. . . . Now, *you* think!" The news director of a San Francisco station says: "We bring things to their attention people hadn't thought about." Two Seattle television stations have been trying editorially to create a climate so that possible racial confrontation, not considered a likelihood in the Northwest, never need occur.

Broadcast editorializing in general may be one thing, while editorializing with courage on touchy subjects may be quite another. With a few notable exceptions, most stations got into the field with some caution, and editorials championing motherhood and demanding fearlessly that Main Street's name be changed to Affluent Way were more the rule than the exception. Some editorializing stations have not progressed very far beyond the safe question even after some experience, but a number have gotten into controversial areas and shown a commendable degree of intestinal fortitude. Since 1960, says Harry Durning, seasoned editorial director of WBZ, Boston, broadcast editorialists have been tackling tougher subjects. His own

65

station's record attests to this. In the last year or two WBZ told its audience editorially: "The taxes you people are paying are not really as high as you think." The station came out against a pay raise referendum for Boston police. It took the negative side on job preference for veterans. WFBM, Indianapolis, repeatedly pointed out the embarrassing truth that while everybody was deploring racial segregation in the South, Indianapolis was living with a sizable amount of de facto segregation in its own schools.

An editorial that might be uncontroversial in one community can be a burning, emotion-packed question in another. When KSTP, St. Paul, plugs for extension of daylight saving time to bring Minnesota into line with the rest of the country, it certainly invites the wrath of the farm community in its signal area. When WDSU, New Orleans, urges full compliance with federal laws on civil rights in the Deep South, the station is unlikely to make friends among the white, conservative element.

Time to reply to a station's editorials is, of course, most likely to be demanded when they are the controversial kind involving strong feelings in the community or among certain groups in the community. Most stations welcome requests for rebuttal from responsible opposition groups, since this gets a dialogue going on the issue, which may heighten public interest. Equivalent airtime is made available, and many stations provide editing help and coaching for the person who reads the rebuttal on the microphone or the camera. Occasionally, a station's bold stand has resulted in court action.

The taking of sides on issues by broadcasters, unequivocally clear in the case of the editorial, involves them in certain government ground rules which their print brethren do not have to worry about. While the FCC encourages stations to editorialize, to express a point of view, the Commission also insists that because of the nature of broadcasting, the station must also air other points of view to provide a balance for its audience. This proposition is embodied in what is known as the FCC's Fairness Doctrine and its effect on the stations in respect to editorials, the endorsements of candidates for office, and other matters will be discussed in a later chapter on the regulation and control of broadcasting.

Some kinds of editorials certainly anger people, but do they make anything happen? It is a rare news director or station manager who will claim that his editorial alone did the job, and often it is very hard to tell. There can be many forces at work, many proponents and opponents, and several sources of pressure contending on a given community issue. The air editorial is only one voice. But there are a number of cases where it is clear that the broadcaster could claim much if not all the credit for results. These will be spelled out with case examples in our chapter on television journalism and the community. But a few basic points can well be made here. Stations find that their audiences listen to and look at their editorials. They pay attention; they react. Stations are applauded or disputed on positions they take by phone, by mail, by word of mouth. Frequently calls come into the station disagreeing with the editorial but praising the station for speaking out.

In reactions to air editorials evidence often appears to support the author's belief that a large segment of the United States public (here called the nonreaders) depends on television and radio for knowledge of what is going on in the world. In a number of cities—all of which have one or more daily newspapers—broadcast managers have been startled to receive calls and letters from people asking: "Tell me. What is this 'editorial' program I get on your station? Just what is an editorial anyway?" There can be no other conclusion than that such people do not read the editorial page of their paper, or if they do, don't know what it is they are reading. This realization—that a segment of the audience is receiving its only opinion on issues via radio and television—points up the importance both of the service provided and the responsibility involved in editorializing on the air.

However, a sense of responsibility, which motivates the practitioners of formal editorializing, leads others to stay away from it. They feel it is not quite right to use their broadcast privileges to state their own personal views. This kind of broadcaster points out that the broadcast editorial is not the only way by which the electronic journalist can draw issues to the attention of the audience, make it think, goad it to action. It is not beyond the power of certain kinds of reporting in depth—as seen in the preceding chapter or of enterprise reporting, which will be touched upon in the next two chapters—to accomplish the same ends. At KMTV, which does not editorialize, they say: "Facts are as eloquent as editorials"; and at WBZ, which does editorialize, they say the presentation of facts in a documentary eventually leads the program into the formulation of a point of view which can have an editorial effect. One station manager explained his philosophy in connection with a specific in-depth treatment as follows: "On the problem of water pollution—rather than putting one man on the air telling people the river should be cleaned up, we put our special department to work on the overall problem and at the end of the film documentary, through the voices of experts who know what they're talking about, the program told our people what needed doing. This in our opinion is the ultimate in editorializing."

SEVEN

COMMENTARY, CONTROVERSY, AND PERSUASION

The broadcaster has no hard and fast rules telling him how much time and money to devote to news and public affairs programming. Nor is there a clear statement of the degree of journalistic responsibility he undertakes, although pressures push him in one direction or another, and general regulations and attitudes emanate from the FCC which bear on the public service he renders to his community. Further, it is possible for the broadcaster to live successfully with a policy of minimum amounts of news and public affairs programming and maximum blandness if he goes beyond the straight presentation of news at all, and complete absence of interpretation, analysis, commentary, or editorializing. Journalistically, such a broadcaster maintains a stance of token commitment.

Another broadcaster may live successfully with a policy of maximum news and public affairs programming. He may grapple with tough, controversial subjects, dig into them, letting the chips fall where they may, and leave no doubt that he is out to make those things happen that he thinks should happen. He is a journalist with a very real commitment. Then a broadcaster may—and a great many do—live with a policy which lies somewhere in between these two. And among these the degree of their commitment most often depends on their approach to what is called in this chapter commentary, controversy, and persuasion. In fact, one school of responsible broadcasters raises an ethical question about whether their role should go beyond reporting the news.

They ask, is television's proper role—outside of its entertainment function—to dissent, to persuade, to commit publicly to a firm point of view? Or is it not to chronicle the events of our day as objectively as possible and leave it to the audience to make its own judgments? It may not be just a question of whether the man who makes the decision—broadcast management—is courageous or cautious. It's a question—so the argument goes—of whether enough men in broadcasting have the wisdom to tell the nation or the community what to do about matters of vital importance; whether with an instrument as powerful as television, the potential for doing harm isn't as much to be considered as the potential for doing good. If one point of view is promulgated, is there not a responsibility to present the other side or sides? But does this not neutralize the effect of taking any point of view at all? As some of the governmental attitudes on broadcasting seem in effect to be asking, is this kind of commitment a suitable role for broadcasters to assume?

There is an honest disagreement on questions like these among broadcasters, which may be summarized in the views of two eminent spokesmen, both newsmen by background. Howard K. Smith says, "Truth is where you find it." He maintains that if the facts show that a position is called for by the journalist, a position should be presented to the audience. Former NBC President Robert Kintner says, "It is not our job to take sides. We should present the story objectively and let the public decide for themselves."

The idea of expressing opinions on the air was first stimulated by traditions established by newspaper columnists, and editorials. In fact, it was to newspaper-trained men like Boake Carter, Fulton Lewis, and H. V. Kaltenborn, that radio turned, and it was they and men like them who were responsible for the heyday of commentators on radio during the thirties. It should be noted that these commentators ran the gamut of the political spectrum in the views they expressed, so that any given network affiliate was likely to produce both a right and a left point of view. Further, this commentary was not identified directly with the broadcast management through whose facilities it was heard.

With the growth of television after World War II, the old commentator days failed to carry over, and instead regular news staffs and staffers began to take positions and express points of view that were clearly those of management or with the approval of management. During the fifties and early sixties—particularly as opinion so labeled, the broadcast editorial, got the FCC's endorsement—the news departments of networks and stations, backed by their managements, assumed in varying degrees the role of national or community conscience and became deliberate persuaders when the situation warranted.

Those who tackle this kind of journalistic responsibility do not share the carte blanche freedom enjoyed by the press. For in taking sides, broadcasters incur a regulatory obligation to present the other side or sides. As mentioned

in the previous chapter, even when it encourages editorializing and the airing of current issues, the FCC requires
that all stations afford a reasonable opportunity for the
expression of views that are in contrast to positions taken
by the station itself or by those who use the station, when
they involve controversial issues of public importance. The
Commission does not require that this be done in exactly
the same number of minutes of exactly equal airtime; it
says that what is involved is the balanced presentation of
issues in view of total programming.

Most broadcasters object to this FCC doctrine, but
although it is a regulation none can ignore, it would not
appear in many cases to have greatly changed the stance
on commentary, controversy, and persuasion which is
really dictated by the broadcaster's own convictions.
Whether the Fairness Doctrine is to some degree at least
an impediment to bold electronic journalism, it seems
clear to the committed electronic journalist that to live up
fully to his potential for informing and enlightening the
American listener and viewer, he must face his audience
with the big issues of the day, and more often than not
these are issues which involve controversy.

One related matter needs to be mentioned at this point.
A fact of life both sides of this ethical argument admit they
have to live with is that not even the prudent journalist is
going to be able to earn himself perfect marks for objectivity. It is probably valid to say that it is beyond the
capability of human kind, of even the good journalist, to
be entirely objective. There would seem to less chance
than otherwise to remain antiseptic in television with its
stinging personalness than in other media of communication. Objectivity is compromised with a raised eyebrow,
a pause, a tone of voice, a three-word aside by the on-air

communicator. The order of scenes shown in the pictorial unfolding of a story, their relative length, the lingering of a camera on a specific shot, the very choice of stories for inclusion in a newscast, constitute an editorial judgment and express a point of view. Whether deliberate or not, any of these things can exert an influence on a viewer, can create a reaction conscious or unconscious that may affect the opinion of the viewer who is supposed to decide for himself.

Neither objectivity nor controversy is an absolute term except in the dictionary definition. What each one means is what a given practitioner has it mean. One man's objectivity may be another man's story with a slant. One man's controversy may be another man's blandness. Certain answers to what is controversial are not to be found simply by measuring the reaction of the target of the message—the audience. A story presented in a manner which the editor considers most objective can bring the charge of prejudice from viewers. Sometimes, a subject controversial by almost any definition may draw no public response at all.

Whether or not a subject is controversial depends on when and where it is dealt with, and whom you're talking to. Birth control is no longer the controversial matter it was a few years ago. Negro voting rights are only regionally controversial. Public welfare is controversial only with the country's conservatives. WFBM, a leading Indianapolis station, blew up a storm by advocating the acceptance of federal aid for education, welfare, and other progressive activities in its predominantly conservative community. Its counterpart in New York, New Orleans, or San Francisco would have brought no such reaction. The American Indian might draw only polite viewer interest as a television subject in most communities. In the state of Oklahoma, where a large minority of the population is Indian, it is a vital matter.

Having determined what is controversy in a particular case, the serious reporter is often still not sure how to deal with the situation. Harry Reasoner, a CBS News correspondent, reflects the dilemma:

> There used to be . . . the idea of objectivity by which if you gave a certain amount of time to one side of the story you gave a certain amount of time or space to the other. This concept of objectivity failed completely. . . . So . . . they changed the old standards of what was objective to include the information available to an intelligent reporter. A reporter is not supposed to report things he knows not to be true without saying they are not true. He is supposed to inform and give background material as well as report what somebody says. And the problem is that these new standards are terribly easy to misuse.[1]

How is controversy being treated today? Critics say that as far as the networks are concerned, the controversy balance sheet looks less healthy than it did a few years ago. It is said that 1964 was the year when documentaries generally turned away from "gut issues" to cultural and feature material. They say that nervous sponsor money and therefore nervous management has brought this about. Richard Doan of the late *New York Herald Tribune* deplores the end of the networks' golden age in public affairs programming and particularly the waning of such programs in prime time. Where are the programs like Rachel Carson's Silent Spring (CBS Reports, 1963)? Here it was obvious that CBS producers shared Miss Carson's sympathies on pest control.

As we have noted about the editorial form of journalism —which the networks generally avoid—the documentary is not the only means of influencing the minds of viewers in controversial areas. Other forms, of course, are commentary, interpretation, and analysis of the news.

Analysis can be defined as a critical examination of the elements of the news; e.g., Ho Chi Minh's message to Pope Paul (February, 1967) was not initiated by the former; it was a reply to the Pope's earlier plea for peace in Vietnam. Ho's conditions for talks called for cessation of all United States military activity in Vietnam as well as the bombing of the north. He offered no reciprocal action by the North Vietnamese.

Interpretation can be defined as giving the meaning of the news. For instance, Ho knows that President Johnson insists on reciprocal action in exchange for stopping the bombing if talks looking toward peace are to take place. So his reply to the Pope means that he has no expectation that talks will come out of it. Furthermore, it means that Ho feels his country has the will and the capacity to continue the fight at least for the time being.

Commentary can be defined as editorial comment, explanation, or criticism of the news. For example, resumption of our bombing in the north may not be enough to change the communists' minds. It seems to me that only a substantial escalation of the war will bring Ho to the conference table.

Any reporter who goes beyond the facts of a story indulges in one or more of these amplifications of the news. Analysis can be achieved with a minimum intrusion of the reporter's own views. Subjective thinking on the reporter's part can but need not creep into interpretation. Commentary clearly involves the reporter's own opinion.

The more conservative analysis and interpretation are widely practiced in one form or another, from a single

sentence added at the close of a reporter's story to a three-
or four-minute "think piece" delivered by a senior correspondent. They make a definite contribution to a viewer's
understanding of the news. Although expression of an editorial view is the natural next step after analysis and interpretation, it requires a more daring news policy, and it is
not very common on the air today. What commentary
there is has a marked effect on the viewer because it provides a greater degree of stimulus to his thinking and to
the formation of concurring or opposing views; the viewer
becomes actively involved.

Commentary is practiced, at least sometimes, at the
national level by a handful of veteran newsmen the networks feel they can entrust with the explicit or implicit
right to express their views on gut issues. These include
Howard K. Smith, Edward P. Morgan, David Brinkley,
and Chet Huntley. Eric Sevareid delivered a half-hour
essay on Vietnam in June, 1966, which Jack Gould of the
Times described as "a step in the right direction of allowing
television correspondents more leeway in advancing their
own opinions and frankly labeling them as such."

At least two group-ownership station systems use commentators. Group W, the Westinghouse stations, have
regular comment from Erwin Canham of the *Christian
Science Monitor*, Rod MacLeish, and Jerry Landay, each
reporting in a field of his special competence. The Corin-
thian stations share the views of Stewart Alsop, Roscoe
Drummond, and Walter Kerr in what they call Columnists
on the air.

The men in Group W's case, at least, are given "professional freedom of subject material and opinion and are
encouraged to exercise it." Their work is intended to
"bridge the gap between news coverage and editorial

position."[2] So we come back to the station level where today the boldness ratio seems to be rising even if it is not doing so at the networks.

A growing number of television stations are embracing controversy. The same motivations which drive a station to editorialize seem to be at work in whatever journalistic form the station uses to grasp disputed issues by the forelock. As noted earlier, some stations take a stand on one side of a community question, even though their position may be an unpopular one. Boston's WBZ in the last few years has carried on a drumfire aimed at chicanery and incompetence in city and state government, as a challenge to a complacent public. In Dallas, a city with a powerful establishment not in the habit of having its prerogatives questioned, station KRLD broadcast a series of debates which gave opposition candidates for the City Council the rare opportunity of wide exposure to the voters. Result: the voters dented the establishment's solid front by electing a member of the opposition. San Francisco's KRON presented a sympathetic documentary on the subject of homosexuals.

One extreme case—a broadcaster whose sense of public responsibility carried him to the point of being forced out of business—has recently gained the admiration and respect of fellow broadcasters as well as the public. In Bogalusa, Louisiana (a Ku Klux Klan stronghold in the Deep South) Ralph Blumberg, the owner-manager of radio station WBOX, undertook an editorial campaign urging community leadership to move actively to bring about peaceful integration of the races. For nearly a year he persisted, withstanding threats on the lives of himself and his family. Eventually the local merchants, upon whom he depended for the economic life of WBOX, were one by one intimidated into boycotting the station, and Blumberg was forced to sell. This broadcaster failed, for the moment, to accomplish what his principles led him to defend. Who can say but that in the long run he has not made a shining contribution to courageous journalism?

When dealing with a controversial subject, a station normally presents either its own side or its own version of the two sides. WSOC, Charlotte, North Carolina, tried a new tack in the spring of 1965. It made the station the producer and vehicle for airing the controversy, but did not serve as a protagonist.

The controversy arose when the Charlotte-Mecklenburg School Board proposed a budget for the coming year allowing for growth in the school system, which required a fifteen-cent increase in the county tax rate. The County Commissioners subsequently laid down a law stating that the tax rate would not be increased. At this point the School Board planned a public meeting with community leaders to try to sell its case. Observers at WSOC, watching these developments, were struck by the fact that the general public was simply not aware of the full import of these developments, and cast about for a way in which the station could help. Their decision was to offer to aid the School Board in presenting its case to the meeting via television. The same offer was made to the Commissioners.

The upshot was that the WSOC staff and the School Board formed a team which delivered, over television, the School Board's presentation to the meeting in the high school auditorium by means of monitor receivers. The program was available, of course, to viewers generally over home receivers all over the community. The station presented no point of view of its own but simply utilized its own facilities and knowledge of the techniques of television to assist the School Board in making its point. The County Commission, which had been offered the same opportunity, did not choose to accept it.

The value of this approach, in the opinion of news director Carroll McGaughey, ". . . was that both sides had the opportunity to make maximum use of television to present their own cases in their own best light without the actual interference of whatever point of view the television station itself may have had." [3] This is, of course, an example of a station performing a community service without taking sides on a strategic controversial issue. WSOC, unlike some stations, did not feel its responsibility was to wind things up by putting the station unmistakably on the line for either the position of the School Board or the County Commission.

The forms of journalism calculated to stir things up—crusading journalism—are not complete without investigative reporting, sometimes called enterprise reporting, which is the kind of digging for facts behind the story or unearthing unknown or only suspected material that results in the exposé—the evidence of skulduggery whose very revelation makes things happen. This is a new departure for broadcast news, but it is showing promise at both the network and the local level. Since this kind of reporting is in effect a making of news, it will be taken up in our next chapter. Let us say here that although it is not an answer for all of the overriding issues we discuss under the heading of commentary, controversy, and persuasion, it is a powerful arm for the broadcast journalist who chooses to make the fur fly rather than simply transmit the news that comes to him through the normal sources available to everyone. If management turns loose a crack news staff, under no taboos, to use the tools of intelligent news selection, hard-hitting, in-depth programming, editorials, and investigative reporting—then the combination gives broadcasting overwhelming power to influence people. Should it exercise so much power?

I firmly believe that it should, for the very reason that television is an immensely powerful medium of communication. And I think it cannot afford to handle controversy with such caution or such artificial treatment that viewpoints cancel each other out. Ed Murrow said: "We have no right to leave people with the impression that every truth has a truth of equal weight on the other side." In today's and tomorrow's world there is too much at stake to duck the big, controversial issues outright or by sitting on the fence. The people in our democracy are the ones to make final decisions, and they must be stirred up and caused to agree or disagree and sometimes made angry and involved in a way that simply doesn't happen when all the pros and cons are given equal time regardless of their merits.

If NBC News strictly practiced what Robert Kintner preached—complete objectivity in news—in this writer's view it would not be stimulating to tune in on, nor would it be a well rounded news service. As a matter of fact, without admitting as much, NBC has set a record of saying what it thinks, as have the other two networks. NBC's first-rank team, Huntley and Brinkley, know how to be objective but they are at their very best when they let us know how they feel about the news.

The electronic journalist, like any journalist, should approach his job soberly and with intelligence. He must know what he is talking about before he takes a stand. But the public should be able to expect that of him today. By the mid 1960s, television journalists are showing that they are wise enough, well enough trained, and responsible enough to do it. In the last analysis, government restrictions such as the Fairness Doctrine should be eased by time if they are in fact a serious hurdle, because the government also must act in the public interest, and response from the public to those broadcasters who demonstrate journalistic guts is beginning to show that this is what the public considers to be its interest.

A deliberate attempt to persuade people to his point of view places an awesome responsibility on the broadcaster. But electronic journalism has passed its childhood. Its practitioners must not shirk the hard, rocky road to the truth as they see it. Let me use the thoughts of two wise and experienced men of broadcasting. First, John Dille, Jr., President of a group of stations and in 1966 Chairman of the Board of the NAB:

Broadcasting can realize a role so dynamic its magnitude is hard to assess only by casting off some of its shackles and inhibitions. Some of these are imposed by self-aggrandizing ownerships or management, some by failure of broadcasters to stand up to the regulators, and some by inertia.[4]

And Norman Swallow, author and independent producer:

The challenge . . . is to seek out matters of public concern and openly condemn them as shameful or praise them as examples of democratic achievement, to avoid the trap of believing that politicians and other public figures are themselves enough, for ultimately the subject-matter of public affairs is people, and they are forgotten at our peril . . . and in view of the importance and power of television, at theirs. But the greatest challenge is to believe that television is also exciting or should be, and to fight staleness and the easy way out with an endless ferocity.[5]

EIGHT

TELEVISION
AS A MAKER
OF NEWS

The program opens with a medium close shot of the news-caster, and he says: "Here is the news!" What follows has the stamp of the news on it, not necessarily for any better reason than that the newsman says it's news. The audience has its mind made up *for* it, and is made party to happenings of the day which are given a life of their own by virtue of a choice made by somebody else. The same judgments are made every day by the editor of the news-paper, but he at least has more space to devote to news stories than the broadcast news editor has time. This is by way of introduction to a journalistic phenomenon more of a factor in radio than in print, more of a factor in television than in radio, in which the medium itself and its prac-titioners become a part of the news they are reporting, have a role in determining what is news, affecting the news they cover, and even by their participation changing the course of human events. This phenomenon is the subject of the current chapter.

The shape of any electronic news show is determined

not only by the choice of what is news but by the emphasis given to different stories and by the way the story is written. The matter of emphasis can be illustrated by the newscast of a small Long Island radio station at the time of the Cuban missile crisis in 1961. The announcer read six stories, all of which concerned the home town of Patchogue —the arrest of a policeman for graft, the announcement of a civil service examination, the opening of a new supermarket. Then he said: "In other news—U. S. Naval vessels today in international waters halted a Soviet cargo ship on her way to Cuba. . . ." An extreme case, but if the station's listeners had no other source of news, what degree of importance would they have placed on the biggest story of the year?

The way the story is written creates a particular impact on the listener. A theoretical example is illustrative. Consider the reporting of a labor-management dispute, and the resulting strike. One writer gives the two sides of the dispute by quoting a spokesman for labor and one for management. Then he devotes a paragraph or a film segment to spelling out the disastrous effect the strike is having on the general public. Another writer quotes the spokesmen, but he follows this part of the story with a paragraph or a film segment depicting the serious plight of the strikers and their families. The final impression on the audience will be quite different in the two cases.

On a Walter Cronkite news program in September, 1966, a story that was given quite a play was the vociferous show of resistance to school integration presented by Boss Leander Perez of Louisiana's Placquemines Parish. It was delivered without any bias on the part of CBS, but the way Perez (and therefore the story) came across, the observer was almost forced to take sides. This story and its editing constituted a comment that could shape audience view-point.

In making the news or at least a side bar to the news, the camera itself is a hero or a villain in the television business. I once watched a late night interview program featuring a guest who came to the studio equipped with his German shepherd dog and a midnight snack. After the dog had been properly admired on the air, he was waved off and the interview began. A whimsical camera-man let his idle camera follow the dog, and suddenly the director of the program perceived on his picture monitor that, unnoticed by his master, doggy was quietly beginning to demolish the midnight snack. The director let the home audience in on the fun by punching the shot up on the air, and at that moment, that was where the news was. The audience could not have cared less what the host and his guest were talking about.

A much more fundamental matter, one fraught with ramifications, is the point at which the medium becomes a participant in the news story—where the story takes a different turn because the medium is present—and here television outdistances all other news media for better or for worse, depending on the kind of event being covered.

Television was a participant in the events surrounding the Kennedy assassination, in that by being there and because of the tone and taste of its coverage it calmed a nation that might have panicked. The emergency of almost any kind that can affect a lot of people is a prime place for radio and television to be an element in the story, a rather constructive element. Much more common than the national emergency is the local emergency brought on by rampaging weather, earthquakes, power failures, armed madmen on the loose—and in such cases it is the local station that becomes an actor in the drama. Acting as extensions of the constituted security, safety, and rescue organs of the area, the stations help keep the populace from losing their heads, but they also become headquarters for collecting and disseminating vital information that gets people to safety, keeps them away from danger areas, and saves human lives.

Stations with well organized news departments in parts of the country subject to hurricanes, tornadoes, or blizzards muster minute-by-minute storm information—not only from all official sources and their own reporters but from dozens of their own listeners and viewers. By staying constantly on the air with the fast breaking story, they provide their communities with the greatest single emergency service—instant communication.

In the electric power failure of 1965 in the northeastern United States, New York radio stations (television was knocked off the air) not only prevented panic; they altered the conduct of people of the city in a way that probably saved more than peace of mind. Jack Gould of the *Times* reported: "Experienced radio people said they could never recall an instance when listeners at home, sensing the plight of stations that were left without normal services from the press associations, pitched in to report on developments or incidents that might provide helpful information for a larger audience." According to the account later in *Newsweek Magazine*, "Listeners were told how to protect refrigerators and oil burners, to beware of frosted food and to stay off the telephone. Wives in the suburbs learned—approximately, anyway—where their husbands were."

Southern California television stations did a comparable job during the massive forest and brush fires that destroyed whole suburban communities in the foothills near Los

Angeles in the fall of 1964. Listeners and viewers have learned to bestow their loyalty and dependence on such stations to an astonishing degree.

There are other and less beneficial ways in which broadcast news becomes a part of the story. One example is the involvement of television correspondents and crews in protest marches or demonstrations. The pro or anti civil rights groups, the pro or anti Vietnam groups, create the news by making their protest in a public place; when television goes out with its cameras to cover this news, it can rarely keep from having an effect on the news.

The reason for this is that protest groups control the time and place and character of the protest, i.e., the news story, and usually their prime purpose is to get widespread dissemination of the story they are creating by television. Television news provides the means of accomplishing what the group most wants, so it is being used when it covers the event. (Professor Daniel Boorstin, University of Chicago, calls this a "pseudo-event.") It is a common experience of stations to receive telephone calls from demonstrators alerting them to what's coming, and in case after case the demonstration begins when the cameras are ready to roll —on cue, as it were.

Demonstrations on vital matters such as civil rights have been in the last few years are news, but the television journalist is a reluctant reporter if he feels that he gives the story artificial weight. When he encounters flagrant cases, the broadcast editor may simply not run the story at all, or omit the pictures in which demonstrators obviously played for the camera's benefit. A Miami film crew found a group of demonstrators sitting on a curb awaiting their arrival before going into their act. The station aired the film but told their audience what the situation was *before* the film was shot. Another point that worries the television newsman is that demonstrations seen on the air tend to put the idea in others' heads, and thus the part television plays in the story is proliferated.

If the peaceful demonstration makes the television man's hair gray, what about the outbreak of violence, the riot? The most prolonged and destructive race riot of our decade took place in the Los Angeles suburb of Watts in August of 1965. For nearly four days, radio and television covered the story and got praise and condemnation for their efforts. Chairman E. William Henry of the FCC warmly applauded the job they did. Others reacted as did John Dunne in the *New Republic*: "With its insatiable appetite for live drama, television turned the riots into some kind of Roman spectacle. . . . Not only did television exacerbate an already inflammatory situation, but also, by turning the riots into a Happening, may have helped prolong them." [1]

The danger of doing just what Mr. Dunne accused them of was present in the minds of responsible television men in Los Angeles. As good newsmen they could not bury or ignore the story. But how to handle it? KTLA provided breathtaking coverage from a camera-equipped helicopter looking down on looting and burning in close-up. The station offered its pictures to its competitors, but some declined to carry them on the ground that they would set an example for others and inflame the already explosive situation. Ultimately, KTLA won awards for its Watts coverage.

How much television influenced developments in the Watts outbreak is hard to assess, but it is significant that the affair caused soul searching among the news fraternity afterwards. Later the same year, there were rumors in

Omaha that a Watts-type uprising was in the making. The radio and television stations—the idea seems to have been arrived at independently at each one—adopted a policy of making no mention on the air of any such possible rioting unless it actually became a fact. The stations of Chicago went even further, agreeing among themselves that they would not air riot stories on television while any riots were actually in progress.

If the questions of coverage and how much coverage by television are recognized as influencing the news, an example of over-coverage was witnessed by a great many Americans. That was the television treatment of President Lyndon Johnson's cold in September of 1964, in which all networks maintained cameras at the hospital over a long period of time, and where bulletins day and night made the country suspicious of the announced medical diagnosis, raising unnecessary alarm over the President's health.

If television in a given instance can change the course or the dimensions of a breaking news episode, it can sometimes do things over a period of time or on a larger scale which can change the very course of events. It can be a participant in the making or the manipulation of history. Television critic John Horn declares that "Television coverage spotlighted the civil rights drive of 1963 into national legislation." Noted commentator Eric Sevareid backs him up with the statement: "The Civil Rights Bill would not have been passed by the Congress when it was had it not been for television." What he was referring to was the nationwide impact of the Negro rights struggle through the early 1960s that was spearheaded by the massive and continuing exposition of it by television. The

89

outstanding social revolution of our day and television's relationship to it merits further examination, which is reserved for our next chapter.

Television and American politics found their way to each other early in the game, and the former has had a profound effect on the latter. Television has changed the forms and content of some of our political folkways, notably our quadrennial national political conventions. In the time that television has been carrying these proceedings to the nation, convention procedures have undergone a streamlining. The order of events has been arranged with television in mind, speeches have been shortened or eliminated, and concessions have been made to accommodate television's hardware that have additionally changed the character of these extravaganzas. As Theodore White put it in *The Making of the President*, ". . . adjustments were made not for the convenience or entertainment of the delegates, but for the convenience of the nation."[2]

A more important effect of television on politics is the part it plays in the campaigns of those running for political office. The man to whom the electronic eye is kind or who can make a telling point over his opponent on the air has the better chance of election. Television in races at all levels of politics has often shown itself to be the element that tips the balance. Theodore White and other analysts of the presidential campaigns of 1960 and 1964 attribute to television a possible decisive role in both races. In both years television figured in campaign gambits, making impressions on the voters which the losing candidates were unable to eradicate or overcome. In 1960 it was the Nixon versus Kennedy debates, in the first of which the Senator came through much more attractively than did the Vice

President. In 1964, three television political spots, two reminding viewers of Senator Goldwater's opposition to a nuclear test ban treaty, the third referring to the Senator's stated opposition to Social Security, were produced by the advertising agency managing Mr. Johnson's television campaign in what Mr. White calls "masterpieces of political television."

The influence of television on the voter reached a new and almost eerie stage in the election of 1964. That was the year in which computer-age election night reporting put the broadcaster in a position where his rapid communicating of returns and of winners could actually affect the conduct of late voters. Due to the time difference across the country, people were still voting on the West Coast after Johnson had been declared President by the networks. Could this lead a voter to stay away from the polls or to change his vote? Studies made since find no evidence that such a thing happened, but the potential is there, and is considered to be a question so serious that a proposal has been made to standardize poll-closing nationally. This concern has been felt and this proposal has been made because of electronic media innovations.

Television's influence over public opinion, or at least over public servants, was pointed out by James Reston of the *New York Times* in connection with the Senate Foreign Affairs Committee hearings on Vietnam. He attributed much of the influence of the Fulbright hearings to the decision of the National Broadcasting Company to televise them. The presence of television cameras in open hearings, in Mr. Reston's opinion, brought added impact on the White House, the Senators involved in the hearings, and on the general public.

Did television play a role of history-making proportions in the murder of Lee Harvey Oswald? It can never be known for certain whether the presence of substantial numbers of television men and amounts of equipment in the basement of the Dallas County Jail on that Sunday morning was what made it possible for Jack Ruby to get close enough to kill the accused assassin of the President. A good many other people besides those of television were crowded into the area. What does seem to be pertinent in the question of television coverage is whether a fair trial for the accused murderer is possible when the act is witnessed by most of the prospective jurors in the country. Seeing a murder committed on television is a rare thing, but it could happen again, and one would certainly have to label it the most incriminating kind of pretrial publicity —an area that has so exercised our courts of law the past few years. Here, however unintentional, television can change the course of events.

A discussion of television's determination of what the news is, its participation in the story, and its actually playing a part in changing the course of events, is not complete without the inclusion of one other facet of the peculiarly close interplay between the medium and the activities it reports. This is the function of television as an originator of news. For a long time the men of television journalism have made news by getting newsmakers to say something newsworthy on the air before they say it anywhere else. With television's growing power, this device has come into widespread usage with the increasing co-operation of public officials and others in the news who find television a most effective vehicle for expressing themselves to the public. One has only to read the newspaper

quotes to see that a substantial number of stories have their origin on the news or public affairs program of a broadcast station or network. The newspaper editor doesn't have a television set in his city room just to look at Batman. He's looking for news breaks and finding them.

With the 1960s, television took a leaf from the book of the enterprising newspaper and tried its hand at investigative reporting—the form of journalism which digs under the surface of the visible news and the news as it appears to be. In discussing the rise of this phenomenon, *Newsweek Magazine* says: ". . . gritty, hard-to-find subsurface news is suddenly coming into camera range." [3] Such work, naturally, often results in revelations that start a chain of events, and thus again places television in the position of moving and shaking through its news operation; of *making* the news.

The best known, and classical, example of the genre was the CBS Reports program, Biography of a Bookie Joint, mentioned in Chapter 5. When producer Jay McMullen and his crew came up with proof that illegal gambling was rife in Beantown and with the permission if not the collusion of the Boston Police, Massachusetts authorities had no alternative but to clean up.

The same redoubtable CBS producer, as head of an investigative unit of the news department, unearthed two stories of national scope, aired on Walter Cronkite's show during 1964. By setting up a fake company, he trapped a number of manufacturers of pep pills into selling him their products, though he had no license to purchase them. With the help of medical men in New York, he then exposed a number of mail order medical laboratories in various parts of the country which were, through carelessness or worse, producing faulty analyses of specimens sent them by their hospital and doctor customers. In both cases, government penalties were applied, and some of the guilty firms went out of business.

The fastest growing investigative reporting is being carried on by local television stations, where some have at least one staffer who spends his time exclusively on this endeavor. Others will detach a man from regular duties when he gets on the trail of something. KMTV, the NBC affiliate in Omaha, sensed something amiss in the construction contract arrangements for a big missile base project at nearby Offut Air Force Base. The station's investigation discovered graft running into millions; the repercussions of its story went all the way to the Pentagon; and the coordinating general for the Offut project was replaced.

An inquisitive reporter for WDSU, New Orleans, dug up the interesting information that a judge of the Louisiana State Supreme Court had never filed a federal income tax return. The judge retired from the bench. WCCO, Minneapolis, broke the story that crooked operators were pocketing public contributions to the Sister Kenny Foundation. The operators went to jail. A man convicted of murder in Texas appealed to a small radio station, whose news staff made its own investigation and developed evidence of the man's innocence. In a ten-month period in 1965, KOGO, the *Time-Life* station in San Diego, claimed to have engineered four exposés, which resulted in the jailing of ten people.

Whether or not this kind of enterprise reporting will get more attention at the network level than it has so far, it definitely will at the station level, as more local stations encourage it. And the success of those who have already gotten their feet wet promises that this more aggressive journalism might be television's most important contribution in the latter half of the sixties.

Television has only recently unveiled its newest toy that makes news, and potentially it is far more than a toy. It can some day be a force to reckon with. This is the national test and instant poll, a kind of journalism where the television audience is the vital participant, where what the audience says is the news.

The first national test was made by CBS in May, 1965, when the nation's drivers were invited to test their skill. Thirty million Americans took the test, the standings of a representative sample being reported while the program was still on the air. The totals—most coming in by mail— were announced a few days later. When millions of people engage in such a test simultaneously, it is news, and this kind of tour de force poses no difficulties for television with its drawing power, its universality, and the speed of its computers. Both NBC and CBS are now involved in the testing game. Tests have been broadcast on national health, citizenship, ethics and honesty, and the income tax. More are coming.

Interesting things are projectable from some pioneering efforts in the area of the instant viewer poll, a vehicle for audience response which can involve questions of greater scope than a viewer test. This concept has had its breaking in at the local level, two stations that have led the way being WTOP in Washington, and WBBM in Chicago.

As with the national testing programs, the strength of the poll is the extraordinarily large number of people who are moved to take part. WBBM drew more than 46,000 responses to a poll program called Feedback, which it aired from nine to ten p.m. on Sunday, November 7, 1965. This one was on the subject of religion, and it made news because it showed that people had some ideas on the subject very different from what church leaders and experts had thought. Here are some of them: a majority of the respondents felt that the church or synagogue should not endorse political candidates or take leadership in social and political actions such as civil rights demonstrations, or on international issues such as United States involvement in Vietnam; 73 percent felt that the church or synagogue should provide sex education for its youth; 69 percent felt that there should be more emphasis on religion in American life; and 61 percent said they would not vote for an atheist for President of the United States even if they thought he was best qualified.

In this form of journalism, as with the instant election returns, television's telescoping of time has significance all its own. Results are a matter of hours rather than days or weeks. To what extent and in what delicate areas of subject matter this may be applied is for the next few years to tell. But the possibilities are profound. Supposing television were to build a massive instant poll around a presidential address, the thrust of which was a big escalation in the Vietnam war. We could have a first-impression reaction representative of the whole American electorate. Predominantly positive or predominantly negative reaction could have repercussions of some consequence on the White House, on Congress or on both. On an explosive issue like civil rights, a strong expression of public opinion one way or the other could conceivably shape at least immediate if not long-range developments on the question, the existing law or governmental policy notwithstanding.

Television is described by some of its proponents as a medium that presents the cutting edge of the news. One might say that the position of television as a force in the news itself—sometimes deliberate, sometimes despite all efforts to avoid it—is the blade, with a two-sided cutting edge. The phenomena discussed in this chapter—phenomena which apply particularly to television—are sobering ones. They envolve heavy responsibilities, and it is fortunate the television newsmen realize it.

NINE

A CASE
HISTORY—
CIVIL RIGHTS
AND TELEVISION

The year 1954 was the time of the momentous Supreme Court decision declaring segregation of the races in public schools unconstitutional, and this act ushered in a period in which civil rights emerged as the most important social issue of our times. That first decision has been followed by a number of significant court decisions and by growing state and national legislation which has had the effect of broadening the legal structure of civil rights protection and eroding the legal structure of segregation. The testing of the growing body of law and court interpretation, and the challenging of the law and its enforcement, have become filled with displays of emotion, hatred, bigotry, hypocrisy, and ugliness that have been a rude shock to the nation. And it is in that area of the searing story that television has found itself to be an extraordinary chronicler of events for the people of America.

Television's cameras and reporters were very much present in the first major clash between federal and local authority when President Eisenhower sent the National

Guard to Little Rock to enforce integration of public schools in 1957, and the public saw what happened over the national networks. Television has been following the civil rights story ever since.

As we turned the corner into the sixties, the days of the freedom riders arrived along with the lunch counter sit-ins in the Deep South and the elaborate machinations of a county in Virginia to thwart school integration. Negro demonstrations brought differing responses from those charged with local and state law enforcement; there was reasonableness and light in some places; there was heat and raw ugliness in others. Television, for the most part, went where the dramatic incidents were and transmitted the sights and sounds of them to its viewers.

In 1962 James Meredith broke the color line at the University of Mississippi when Governor Ross Barnett challenged the authority of the United States, and President Kennedy sent the U. S. marshals to Oxford. Radio, television, and the press covered this grim incident intensively—a newsman lost his life in line of duty—and later the Justice Department was to use television's pictures to disprove the persistent claims that it was the marshals who started the rioting on the campus.

The following year the President was confronted with another recalcitrant governor—George Wallace of Alabama—and names of cities like Birmingham, St. Augustine, and Cambridge, Maryland were in the racial news. But of greater lasting significance in this year was the point at which the civil rights revolution reached national proportions. Northern television newsmen did not have to travel south to find a dramatic or high-tension story—it was breaking out in their own backyard. In the summer of 1963 there were incidents in 220 cities, many a long way

99

from the Deep South. And the audience was faced with the hard truth that no place was exempt from Negro protest and no community had a clean bill of health. Television devoted massive facilities and airtime to covering the march on Washington in August—a unique and orderly demonstration that brought participants from many states north of the Mason-Dixon line. And on Labor Day evening, the NBC network broadcast a three-hour, prime time documentary titled, The American Revolution of '63. It cost the network half a million dollars in revenue from cancelled programs that night.

Although this magnum opus was in a class by itself, other telecasters too were tackling the job of reporting America's number one domestic story in depth. ABC produced a special documentary on the confrontation of federal and local authority in the persons of John F. Kennedy and George Wallace of Alabama. The same network did a five-part series, Crucial Summer, while CBS broadcast Who Speaks for Birmingham? and The Ku Klux Klan—the Invisible Empire. Programs of interview and discussion like Meet the Press and Face the Nation were giving full attention to the civil rights issues, with a broad spectrum of spokesmen as guests. Radio and television stations were taking up the controversies editorially in an effort to calm, to arouse, or to reason with their audiences.

But day after day it was the dramatic surface eruptions that television documented on its regular news programs that kept the story in the national consciousness. In 1964 there were riots in Harlem; Chicago; Athens, Georgia; and Philadelphia, Mississippi. In 1965 the worst riot of them all occurred in Watts—not in the South but in metropolitan Los Angeles. In the South, this was the year of the march from Selma to Montgomery, the murder of civil rights workers, and the massive effort to get Negroes registered to vote.

In 1966 James Meredith went back to Mississippi, and in a march to Jackson was shot and wounded for his efforts. Other rights workers carried on. Chicago rioting made the headlines again and there were other names—Omaha, Dayton, Cleveland, and Benton Harbor, Michigan. In Watts, a year after the holocaust, a Negro was killed by a policeman and tension returned to the scene. The coroner's inquest to determine whether it was deliberate or accidental homicide was covered live by television station KTLA. The district attorney welcomed the coverage so that "all can see the investigation is being conducted in a fair and impartial manner." The authorities and other observers agreed that this access to the inquest for hundreds of angry residents of Watts may well have headed off new violence.

During the decade of revolution since Little Rock, television journalism and the civil rights movement have been closely linked. Television has had a profound effect on the revolution of the nonwhite, and the revolution has had an effect on television, too. Let's look at the effect on the medium and its newsmen wrought by the movement and the Negro himself. First, the electronic medium has, in a real sense, been used by the "revolutionaries."

William Monroe, a native of the Deep South, veteran newsman and now chief of the NBC News Bureau in Washington, explains this well:

The Negroes are the architects, the bricklayers, carpenters and welders of this revolution. Television is their chosen instrument.

Not because television set out to integrate the nation or even improve the South. But, because, when the Negroes got ready for their revolution, television was there. Television was coming of age as a journalistic medium; it was, unlike the newspapers, a national medium; it had the courage, in most cases, a courage drawn from the old tradition of the American press, not to shrink from the fierce and often ugly scenes growing out of the Negro struggle; and it conveyed the emotional values of a basically emotional context with a richness and fidelity never before achieved in mass communications.[1]

From the television newsman's point of view, Bill adds:

The story was there, so we covered it as a sort of automatic reflex, without intending that the coverage should have any influence on the events and without much thought about what effects the coverage might have.[2]

But because it was clear to television that it was a part of the story, and because when newsmen got into it they saw how important the story was and how difficult it was to cover objectively owing to its highly emotional nature, the television journalists have made a hard effort to maintain reportorial integrity. There have been instances—particularly earlier in the game—when television men encouraged demonstrators to act for the cameras. Putting a violent moment into its proper context is a tenet of reporting not always adhered to. The problem of how to get a reasonable spokesman of the southern whites to come before the cameras is a tough one. So is the frequently puzzling matter of who it is who really speaks for the Negro.

Soul searching, experience through the years of crisis, learning by mistakes, have given network newsmen—the principal conveyors of the national story—a sound grasp of this piece of history-in-the-making and how their medium should handle it to inform and enlighten the public. They have deployed able manpower—including staffers from the South—wherever the events of the story required it. They have in some cases acquired valuable perspective from station newsmen close to the local scene, particularly in parts of the South. They have assigned painstaking newsmen to the production of documentary programs and other in-depth examinations of the race crisis. Television camera teams—often themselves targets of hatred when they appeared on the scene of demonstration or violence—have comported themselves with courage and enterprise, even though some of them at times got carried away with the story. This will be discussed at the close of this chapter.

Television has been affected by the civil rights struggle it has been reporting, to an extent that may be hard to measure, at least for another few years. I am inclined to agree with Bill Monroe's estimate:

I would guess that the racial story, even more than the space shots, the political conventions and the Kennedy assassination, has helped elevision find itself, not only as a powerful technical instrument, but as a journalistic medium of maturity and guts —one capable of adding to the vigor of a huge democracy.[2]

Anyone who watches television news must have at least a strong suspicion that the medium must have played a part in the steps the Negro is making toward equality. Again I quote Monroe:

The consensus of people I've talked to about the subject is that television has been a central factor in the development of the Negro revolution . . . has accelerated it and forced a much speedier confrontation of emotion and ideas than otherwise would have been the case. That is certainly my own belief.[2]

Of course, television had different impacts and stirred different feelings in different segments of its audience. The principal segments of interest here are those of the southern white, the southern Negro, whites outside the South, and the ghettoed nonwhite of the North and West.

Mr. Monroe says about the white southern audience:

The first time many southern whites saw southern Negroes standing up and talking about their rights was on network television. They just plain didn't believe it. Some of them still don't. Some of them are still convinced that the networks are manufacturing these unbelievable Negroes. Network television, a new national medium with a determination to cover the news, broke through the magnolia curtain. The segregationist south was shocked. [And many hours of television news programs later, as Bill Monroe put it] Gradually, slowly, painfully, as the pictures kept coming, the idea began to dawn that integration *was* inevitable, that the Negroes *were* changing, that the federal government was too big, that there was nothing the South could do about it.[2]

Television did two things for the southern Negro. Mr. Monroe vividly describes one of them:

It has brought the outside world to Negroes in thousands of southern towns and cities. The signals went out from the TV towers in Atlanta, Memphis, Birmingham, Mobile, Jackson, Shreveport, Richmond, and Charleston to hundreds of thousands of shacks and houses with leaky roofs and unpainted sides—and television antennas on the roof. And inside them at twilight the Negro families watched the network newscasts originating from Washington and New York—in most cases, the only daily news source they trusted. The Negroes in Mississippi watched the sit-in demonstrators in Tennessee and the freedom riders pushing into Alabama. And many of them who couldn't read could watch and listen as Presidents of the United States talked on television about civil rights and registering to vote.[2]

A second thing television did for Negroes, especially the isolated Negro of the South, was to let them see, in entertainment programs and television commercial messages, a world they weren't a part of. Sociologist S. I. Hayakawa points out, "Whatever the television set says to white people, it also says to Negroes. The Negro discovers when he shops for clothes, eats at lunch counters and so on that the culture is not willing to live up to its advertising." [3] And so the sense of deprivation, the arousal of unfulfilled expectations made graphically clear by television, goads the Negro to make his fight for civil rights.

The impact of television on whites outside the South came in two waves involving two differing sets of emotions. First, the on-the-scene coverage of intimidation and bestiality in the five southern tier states of the old South made indelible impressions on many who had been oblivious to or indifferent over home-grown, American brutality and injustice. Suddenly men and women all over the country were as close as across the street to the crucible of revolution. Whites everywhere were awakened and shaken up.

The second wave was occasioned by the spread of Negro protest in cities large and small over much of the nation outside the South. Now white viewers who had been revolted at the injustice and critical of the southern white had to look at the powder keg on which they too were sitting, and face the fact that though the methods of achieving discrimination and maintaining segregation might be entirely different, in effect discrimination and de facto segregation existed all around them.

Negroes living outside the South have been constant observers, and many of them participants, in the war being waged by their brethren in the South. Over television they have seen and heard their cause articulated by the James Baldwins and Martin Luther Kings and James Farmers of their race. They have noted the legislation and the court decisions which mark on paper at least the provisions for their first-class citizenship. Their reaction to what they consider the wide gap between what is promised and what they are getting has brought eruptions in the North which in their turn have been faithfully disseminated to all by television. They too have been affected by the reflection television provides of today's affluent society in which most of them do not participate.

Television's coverage of the civil rights story, deliberately or not, was interpreted as saying different things to different people, and in sum has been responsible for an inestimable number of developments in the story itself. The knowledgeable commentators in the field are in agreement that the most important national legislation to date —the Civil Rights Act of 1964—was brought about, or at least was brought about when it was, as a result of pressure which television engendered. In speaking of television's role in an even bigger context than the civil rights struggle alone, Eric Sevareid says:

The nation has come to think automatically in terms of social progress, of a better life for all. Television may well have been a critical prod to America's conscience and the spur to Congressional action. . . . Civil rights, unemployment, poverty and ignorance . . . people are ready for these actions by government, and one reason may well be fifteen years of a new kind of mass communication, the intimate impact of television.[4]

The implications of all this are not lost on the White House, which from Eisenhower's day on has had to be an occasional active participant and a constant force in the background of the struggle for civil rights. President Lyndon Johnson, a close watcher of television himself and a highly political person, pays close attention to the signs and portents arising from the impact made on Americans by the electronic eye.

Before we leave this story of the interaction of a news medium and a social revolution, something more should be said about the charges of unfairness that have been made against the press, including television. At a Senate Committee hearing a few years ago, Senator Strom Thurmond of South Carolina told the President of CBS, Frank Stanton, that his network systematically distorts the issue by emphasizing the Negro case and subordinating the white southern point of view. He and others have charged that the convictions of thoughtful people in the South have not been communicated to the country at large, and that by playing up the racial conflict, unstable elements and publicity-seekers are supported and aid and comfort is given to the Communists.

A responsible television news director in Dallas told me that when he offered his network a story on the peaceful integration of the schools of Fort Worth, Texas, it was turned down because there were no demonstrations or episodes of violence to report. He felt that it was the very absence of these things which made it news, but that New York was not interested in crediting a southern community with peaceful integration.

Some claim that the dramatic eruption of racial trouble beginning several years ago which was a sharp shock to Americans nearly everywhere reflects on American journalism—television included; that what was coming was obvious in advance, and responsible journalism could have prepared the people for it. Whether this charge can be sustained is beyond this author to say, but there does seem to be evidence that a good segment of television was remiss in not turning the attention of people outside the South to the short fuse burning in their own communities, until the bomb went off.

Joseph Brechner, a Florida broadcaster who has covered the civil rights story himself and carried the coverage provided by his network, recently spoke to this question and at the same time another which critics have raised. This question was, "Does national coverage of racial strife incite further incidents and demonstrations, and does it intensify these conflicts?" "This may be so," says Mr. Brechner, "but I'm not willing to accept the alternative— a news blackout." And he goes on:

The outbreak of violence into major news event proportions requiring federal troops to maintain law and order came as an incredible surprise to most Americans. With no safety valve or warning device, we were all sprayed by the scalding racial steam when this boiler exploded in our faces. Our nation had not been sufficiently exposed earlier to these simmering conflicts, nor arrived at a conscious realization of our local and national neglect of these problems. When the crises arrived, many white Americans were shocked. To justify self-righteousness they looked for scapegoats and blamed the Negroes for creating issues inducing white violence. It was like condemning the victim for his own murder. No, the problem is not too much coverage, but belated coverage.[5]

Through the years of the civil rights story, the question has been raised concerning the behavior of some southern broadcasters as well as newspapermen in the handling of the story. Research for this book has not been intensive enough in this area to pin the question down accurately. There is no doubt that a number of radio and television stations in the Deep South have done a fair and courageous job of reporting, some have even editorialized with a voice of reason which must have alienated white extremists.

The case of Ralph Blumberg with his station WBOX, Bogalusa, is a living example of this. There is one case of a southern station which is openly accused of anti-Negro prejudice and whose license is now under government review.

When the license of station WLBT, Jackson, Mississippi, came up for renewal in 1965, the FCC was petitioned (actually in 1964) by the Office of Communications of the United Church of Christ to deny the renewal application and to order hearings at which the petitioner could present evidence that the station was guilty of racial and religious discrimination and excessive commercialism. The FCC turned down the petition and renewed the station's license for one (instead of the usual three) years—a restricted and conditional renewal.

The Reverend Everett C. Parker, Director of the church office, appealed the FCC decision to the federal court. In March of 1966, the U. S. Court of Appeals, District of Columbia, held that the Commission had erred in renewing the license while ignoring the church's—representing the station's public—petition to be heard. The Commission ordered that the hearing be held.

TEN

ELECTRONIC
JOURNALISM
IN THE
COMMUNITY

The prominence of the place occupied by a good radio or television news station in its own community is only beginning to be generally recognized, although its standing with its own audiences is so well established that it is almost taken for granted. Stations that have been operating for a long time are aware that they have audiences that swear by them. Those stations—particularly in television—which have only recently invested in substantial news services are beginning to sense the depth of the impression such services can make for them in their signal area. And now broadcast critics, newspapers, sociologists, and public officials are paying attention.

So far as ownership goes there are three kinds of broadcast stations—those owned as single entities, those owned as part of a group, those owned by the three national networks. The law allows an individual, partnership or corporate ownership of as many as five VHF (Channels 2 through 13) television stations, so long as they are in different markets. Each of the three major networks owns and operates five. Other group owners, not operators of networks, own anywhere from two to five VHF stations; some own UHF (Channels 14 through 83) stations also. Most group stations are affiliated with national networks, but their affiliations are mixed. The *Time-Life* station in Indianapolis, for example, is an NBC affiliate; the one in Denver is a CBS affiliate. The network O & O (Owned and Operated) stations and the group ownership stations maintain some of the most enterprising and best news establishments in the country. They have generally set the standards that serve as models for other stations.

Whether a station is owned by a network, affiliated with a network, or independent, and whatever national news programs it may carry produced by others in New York or Washington or overseas, what gives each station its individuality is the news job it does with its own hands. For many television stations, news and public affairs are the only programs of any kind produced in its studios and with its remote (live) or film cameras. Led by its news department, the station is of a piece with its community like the local newspaper, the supermarket, the utility companies, and the big electronic parts plant on the outskirts of town. Its newsmen as well as its management are immersed in community affairs along with the businessman, the banker, the labor leader, and the public servant.

The men of the station's non-entertainment services know their community, its people, its needs, and its problems. They serve the people and the needs and they confront the problems. With their enterprise, their editorials, their investigative work, and their high news standards, the best stations are clearly demonstrating community responsibility. News Director John Corporon of WDSU, New Orleans, says: "We are the community watchdog."

News directors at KING in Seattle and WXYZ in Detroit say that their management's query "What needs doing in this community" is a criterion for action. Reflecting an awareness of the size of the responsibility falling on the television news executive, Dale Clark of WAGA, Atlanta, says: "We have a big impact on local affairs, and we must have tremendous maturity to be entrusted with that impact. The power of TV to educate people must be wielded by men of great integrity."

Let us take up in turn the journalistic forms described in Chapters 3, 4, 5, and 6, and show how in each of these, leading television stations relate to viewers in their own home cities. In the first—live, as-it-happens news—it was pointed out that this is primarily a function associated with networks. But when the occasion demands it, live programming provides a service second to none at the local level. And the occasion is most often the local emergency, the event that occurs with little or no warning that spells danger.

We indicated in Chapter 4 how the local station actually takes part in the story in an emergency. Now let's examine a few cases which illustrate station services and the community dependence on them.

In January, 1966, New York—the United States city least able to cope with it—had a week-long shutdown of its public transportation. Private cars, two-wheeled vehicles, and shanks' mare were the only means of getting through the city. Though little, if any, loss of life could be attributed to the strike, the traffic situation was chaotic. New York television stations blanketed the town with live cameras and with reporters who kept the populace informed by word and picture from every newsworthy location.

San Francisco Bay area stations gave their audiences a running, graphic account of the serious student disturbances on the Berkeley campus of the University of California in 1964.

In the early afternoon of June 16, 1966, two oil tankers collided near Staten Island, New York. The volatile cargo of one of them caught fire and 21 seamen lost their lives. While the fire was still raging and possibly endangering more lives, WCBS-TV got a camera on the air from its mobile truck on a bridge at the scene, and New Yorkers got a live look at the conflagration.

In August, 1965, an explosion occurred at the Du Pont Company's plant on the edge of Louisville, Kentucky. The shock was heard and felt all over town. Station WHAS moved a camera into the explosion area before police and fire authorities had cordoned it off. The television men were ordered to move back, but the crew left the camera behind, trained on the plant. A later explosion was seen as it happened by WHAS viewers.

In all these cases, the television coverage did more than satisfy viewer curiosity. By letting viewers see for themselves what was happening, it kept the event from being blown out of all proportion by fertile imaginations and unfounded rumors.

That such service is appreciated is shown by audience response to the emergency service provided by radio in the New York power failure mentioned earlier in this book. Station WCBS clocked 11,000 telephone calls from listeners during the night, WOR estimated between 5,000 and 10,000. These calls were not just thank-you's or inquiries. Many were calls offering information and services—volunteers helping the radio newsmen to do their job.

Nature can assail man with some of his most terrifying emergencies, and the newsmen of KMTV, Omaha, will long remember one such instance on June 16, 1964. At dusk, a massive cloudburst struck the city and its environs and dropped an incredible nine inches of rain in slightly more than one hour. KMTV crews set out to get what film they could in the darkness. Through its reporters, the newsroom quickly discovered something not yet realized by the city's safety authorities—that in some suburban areas the runoff from the cloudburst had created a death-dealing flash flood. The authorities went into action while the station by voice report and picture warned its constituents of what was going on. Lives were lost that night, but no doubt a lot were saved by an alert station.

Many things are required to enable a broadcaster to serve effectively in this kind of emergency. It takes a careful plan in advance to meet any of a number of kinds of dangerous spasms of nature. It takes a staff, instructed and trained so that they respond instantly and coolly. It takes confidence vested in the station by the authorities to have the necessary mutual cooperation. And above all it takes a high degree of believability by the community in what the station says—built up painstakingly over a period of time—so that the people the station is trying to help will trust it and participate in its effort.

Such was the situation on an evening in June, 1966, when the newsroom of WIBW, in Topeka, Kansas, heard first reports of an approaching tornado given by one of the station's own men. The station flashed the first public warning to take cover 25 minutes before the twister slashed through the city, killing seventeen and causing a hundred million dollars' worth of property damage. Power was knocked out by the blow, but WIBW's radio and television auxiliary transmitters carried on through the night, issuing calls for off-duty police, medical personnel, and National Guard units. It listed emergency shelters and aired personal messages. It calmed the people of the stricken city. Observers say the station's work that night was the principal factor in preventing panic and in keeping the death toll at seventeen.

In September, 1965, two of the three television stations in Miami had their facilities knocked out by Hurricane Betsy. The third, WTVJ, was on the air for 68 consecutive hours while southern Florida was taking the brunt of the storm. The station operated under an emergency hurricane plan, plotted long before. Newsmen were deployed on Miami Beach, the Lower and Upper Keys, Key Biscayne, and at Nassau (Bahamas). Two counties outside Miami were covered, too, and live feeds were made from the station's Fort Lauderdale studio.

Each hurricane report began with the latest from the Weather Bureau's National Hurricane Center in Coral Gables. This was followed by WTVJ's own weather man, Bob Weaver, broadcasting from downtown Miami studios with illustrations and further explanations of the storm. Film from newsmen in the field was rushed in and aired. Live pictures from Fort Lauderdale showed the raging ocean from the seventh floor studio on the shore. The station didn't forget its large Spanish speaking population. It produced an hourly report in Spanish. This WTVJ performance, which has its counterparts in other hurricane-prone areas, proved again the indispensability of the electronic media to authorities and to the public in time of crisis.

WCCO Radio in Minneapolis has been in business since 1924, and has built up through the years an enviable position as a bulwark of strength for the citizens of its community when trouble comes. The station has set records for superlative service in tornadoes and floods, but this account of a side-bar story on the night of a blizzard in March, 1965, perhaps illustrates best the personal relationship which can be found between a station and its listeners.

As the enormous white blanket swept in to begin paralyzing most of a three-state area, a car going east on a secondary road about eight miles out of St. Cloud, Minnesota, crept down into a small, remote valley and couldn't make it up the other side. The driver was not the only misguided traveler on the road. In turn, seven more vehicles piled up behind the first car, and within minutes all were pinned down by the drifting snow.

There was not a house within miles, or a place to take shelter. But the stranded group had two things in its favor. All were natives and knew how to act in this kind of circumstance, and one of the cars belonged to a radio "ham" whose equipment was on hand and in working order. Everyone crowded into a couple of cars—heaters going—to conserve gasoline and the ham began calling for help.

Adverse weather conditions apparently prevented any fellow ham in the region from hearing the call, but at length the stranded party did find a friend through the ether—a shortwave operator in New Jersey, over a thousand miles away. He noted the details, a description of the spot where the cars were marooned, the road number, and the approximate mileage from St. Cloud, and undertook to relay the message. Nobody from Minnesota answered the New Jersey call, but a ham in Florida did. It was from Florida that news of the plight of the travelers first reached the Minneapolis area, where it was received by an operator in the suburbs who promptly phoned—not the authorities but radio station WCCO.

WCCO, which had been broadcasting emergency messages for some hours, got through by long distance phone to the sheriff of St. Cloud, and he put a snow plow on the road, headed for the scene of the tie-up. Then the station told the story on the air. The marooned travelers heard it on their car radios and were cheered. Someone else in the area heard it too—a farmer holed up in his isolated farmhouse listening to the description of the place and recognizing it as being a few miles from him down the valley. He donned his heavy clothing and started out to find the party.

It took the man a couple of hours, but by following his fence lines through the blinding snow and darkness, he got to the cars, now buried in drifts. He found the travelers in good shape and anticipating rescue. They at first declined the farmer's invitation to mush through the storm and take refuge at his house. But before the good Samaritan went his way, WCCO was coming through the car radio speakers with a dismaying report. The plow out of St. Cloud had run into trouble and had to turn back. It just could not get through the drifts. The people in the stranded cars had a sudden change of heart and made ready to go up the fence line with their farmer host.

It was near dawn when WCCO received a phone call from the farmer. He had the party safely around his fire, with blankets and food. The station newsman asked whether the hike through the drifts had been a bad one for the erstwhile motorists. "Not bad," said the farmer. "We *did* have to carry three of 'em the last part of the way."

In the realm of the local station's regular news programs as discussed in Chapter 4, it might be added here that there exists the same kind of neighborly feeling on the part of viewers and listeners as is so dramatically apparent when emergency conditions obtain. A favorite airman—he who anchors the evening or 10 or 11 P.M. local newscast, or covers the news all over town every day—is as accepted a person as the minister, the priest, the teacher, or the postman. Whether they have met him or not, viewers feel that they know him personally. Helpful citizens phone broadcast newsrooms with tips on the news. What people see and hear from him when they tune in the news is to them gospel truth. In New York, a television newsman named Gabe Pressman brings the atmosphere of a small town to the nation's largest city. A 13-year veteran at NBC, he is recognized and spoken to wherever his reporter's rounds take him in the five boroughs.

And people certainly watch local news programs. Jon Poston at KTIV in Sioux City ranks as number four among the top twenty programs in his viewing area with his ten o'clock nightly news show. One NBC affiliate's "News at Noon" takes the measure of a soap opera on CBS, which is on at the same time. There will be more about the pulling power of television's new breed of journalists in Chapter 12.

Programming in-depth, usually on local subjects, stretches the facilities of the local newsroom, but a surprising number of stations manage to turn out good documentaries at least now and then, and some of them bring community action. Seattle's KING delivered one ninety minutes long on the subject of needs for renewal of the port; it was followed up with a town meeting. Both aimed at supporting a ten-million-dollar bond issue, which was subsequently adopted. KBOI in Boise, Idaho did a prize-winning documentary on water pollution, which was followed by action in several Idaho towns and a change in the state law. A series was carried on KMTV's news programs showing the need for flood control measures. The Technical Committee of the local Watershed Board took the matter under study.

Just before Sacramento was to be opened as a deep water port, KCRA had cameras in Europe for three weeks shooting a twenty-part documentary to show the home community the international ramifications of the event. WAGA made the people of Atlanta take a close-up look at their slums. WTVJ, Miami, spotlighted the life of the refugee Cubans in its midst with The Plight of Pepito. Sioux City, Iowa did a special on a vital local matter, the cattle market crash. WHAS filmed the physical aspects of a conservation problem in eastern Kentucky, and after the broadcast showed the film to the state legislators. State conservation officials give the station credit for corrective changes in the state law. Three San Francisco television stations undertook an educational job on potential race troubles which has contributed to understanding and mostly peaceful change in that part of the country. WBZ, Boston, with a series of documentaries concerned with government reform, brought a climate of improvement even without editorial comment.

It is our fourth journalistic form—the editorial—which is the most direct method by which a station, as KOGO put it, "deals itself into" the shaping of community life, and there are an ample number of cases available to show that it works. First, some indications of why it works. Politicians, ever sensitive to powerful voices in their constituencies, pay close heed to station editorials. A number of state governors and city mayors make it their business to know what their stations are saying in editorials. Dick Cheverton, News Director of WOOD in Grand Rapids, reports that officials telephone to ask: "Are you going to editorialize if we do so and so?" And his is not the only town where this happens. If they are a little nervous about broadcast editorials, shrewd politicos are often privately pleased with them because they often deal with subjects the politicians want to see brought up but do not want to bring up themselves. They get a chance to watch the straws in the wind.

From the record of editorial accomplishment—and the speediness of results—it is clear that the power structure of the community reacts to a strong editorial position, if it is validly based, without waiting to see how big a ground-swell will be created by it among the citizens at large. In a sense, if the editorial reaches the people in a position to do something about the issue it raises, it is not too important how many other people it reaches.

The list of stations who have appointed themselves movers and shakers in their towns is growing, and so is the record of their accomplishments. WJBK, Detroit, was the one media voice to speak out against a police civilian review board in half a dozen editorials. The Mayor got six thousand letters from viewers. The measure died. Competitor station, WXYZ, asked why with a rising record of motorcycle accidents in Michigan there was no driver's test required of motorcyclists. The authorities took the cue. WDSU, New Orleans, raised a cry when a group of the Louisiana Governor's friends chartered a new bank under extraordinarily favorable conditions. Corrective action followed in Baton Rouge. WSB, Atlanta, in two separate editorial programs, Comment and Report— neither was actually an editorial—drew attention to a school principal who was charging ten cents for a free school lunch. Children who did not have a dime were doing without. It seemed the school principal wanted to balance his budget more than he wanted to see the children fed. Result: the Superintendant of Schools made it plain to the principal that feeding the children was more important than balancing his lunchroom budget. The children were fed.

KWTV endorsed Oklahoma City candidates for mayor and City Council. All were elected. A pioneer radio editorializer, WMCA in New York, ran a long, costly, and hard-hitting campaign for election district reapportionment for the New York State Legislature. Owner-manager R. Peter Straus paid out of his own pocket to carry the battle into the courts, finally achieving victory in the U. S. Supreme Court, with the one man, one vote decision. In a sterling job of investigative reporting, WJXT, Jacksonville, Florida, broke the story of political influence and corruption in the police department, warned voters the local school system was endangered by the town's tax-assessment formula, and revealed that in failing to offer some contracts for public bidding, the city was violating its own charter. A grand jury investigation has already issued more than a hundred indictments, and an investigative committee has been set up.

WCCO, Minneapolis, uncovered the fact that local prostitution was run by a syndicate. A grand jury swung into action on that one. WGN, Chicago, swam against the newspaper editorial tide with a documentary which showed that the Cook County Hospital was not a hopeless case. The station is given credit for saving the hospital. To give its fellow Texans some sober second thoughts about unrestricted access to firearms, KPRC in Houston stooped to a little skulduggery. They got an eleven-year-old boy to order a German luger by mail and had him use the name of a man on the ten-most-wanted list of the FBI. The station at least made its point.

No station wants to alienate the police department in its town; it is often an important ally. But WTVJ, Miami, with heavy heart, editorialized on a matter to which their news digging had brought them—bribe-taking by local cops. KSTP, St. Paul, did not have to call it an editorial when they publicized what looked to them like deliberate delays by the state legislature to carry its session into overtime and extra pay for all hands. Beginning with the first over-time day, the KSTP news program showed a scoreboard of what that day had cost the taxpayers. The legislature wrapped up its business in a hurry. In establishment-run Dallas, it took courage for KRLD to be the only one to ask what had happened to a rather grim report on Dallas crime which seemed to have disappeared from public view. Belatedly the press took up the question, and out of it came a grand jury investigation.

Every community has its problems, and though some problems are common ones others are peculiar to a partic-ular community. The station which expects to serve its area has to know its community thoroughly, must find where the weak spots are, must know how to deal with them on terms the community understands. When Don Brice, News Director of KPIX, first came to San Francisco he admits to the preconceived notion that he was in a highly sophisticated community and had to shape his news policies accordingly. "I was wrong," says Don. "It may have been true once, and perhaps still is on Nob Hill, but the overall population of the Bay Area these days is far from sophisticated." When a *Time-Life* man from New York visited the *Time-Life* station in Grand Rapids, he was puzzled by what he saw and heard on its news programs. "That," explained News Director Cheverton, "is because you don't know the people of Western Michigan." The emphasis in the newscasts was on the undramatic stuff of local government and local problems, not often lively or even visual fare. It seemed dull to the New Yorker, but by knowing his community, Cheverton knew this was the story his people were most interested in.

Los Angeles television stations, which carry more hours of news than almost any place, have found that the people of Southern California are always news-hungry. The broadcasters don't quite know why, but they go ahead and fill the demand. Deacon Anderson at KING finds Seattle a quiet, conservative place, but he thinks such a situation fosters complacency and feels the media there must fight against this condition. Miami has a growing Cuban population. It also has a growing population of retired people. The television newsman has both to think about. In Detroit, everything revolves around the motor industry; in some Deep South communities, the race question; and in Idaho, potatoes and water. Boston is a hard place for a news organization to know how to serve, according to the men at WBZ. How do you bridge the gap in a town that has its share of uneducated and unskilled at one end, and 32,000 Ph.D.s at the other? But the news staffs at the best television stations in highly diversified communities seem to be serving them well.

Local television, Ernie Schultz of WKY, Oklahoma City, says, is "a tremendous force—a growing force." Herb Robinson, a *Seattle Times* man, who went into television news and is now back at the *Times*, states that the parochialism of his city was changed by television. KTIV, Sioux City, which reaches people in northeastern Nebraska as well as western Iowa, is given credit for making Siouxland—Sioux City's natural rural environs—a cohesive unit. Without local television the periphery areas would lose their affinity to the urban center. News Director Bob Gamble of Indianapolis says that since the Indianapolis press did not do the job of shaking the community loose from its nineteenth-century thinking, Indianapolis television had to do it, and did.

Television newsmen, proud of their position and perhaps guilty of a certain self-serving bias, say things like this: in Detroit—the station's personality is its news; in Sacramento—news is our community individuality; in Sioux City—news gives the station its image. But their judgment is backed up by what viewers say: "To us station X is more than a community institution. It's a *person*." "Station Y is a leader in community action." "Station Z is a *member* of this community."

It seems eminently clear that the job the best local stations are doing today in electronic journalism has earned them extraordinary loyalty and trust from their audiences. It did not happen overnight, and it could not come out of a shoddy product or abuse of responsibility. It represents, I believe, one of the most exciting and positive developments in the story of commercial television in the United States.

ELEVEN

FORCES
WHICH INHIBIT
BROADCAST
JOURNALISM

There are forces which potentially or actually impinge on
the broadcast newsman's freedom to serve his audience
independently of all curbs save his own concept of journalistic integrity. If any or some of these forces affect what
the audience receives, and there is no doubt that they do,
then some knowledge of what they are and how much they
interfere with the newsman's freedom is essential to an
understanding and a realistic evaluation of the final
product.

Among the real or theoretical encroachments faced by
the electronic journalist are a number that he has in common with the newspaper journalist. First, there is the
policy of the man or men who pay his salary—top management or the person or body top management reports to,
i.e., ownership. The owner may call for a bold editorial
course, or a bland one designed to make nobody unhappy.
He may seek to inject his own personal prejudices into the
news product; he may adopt news policies calculated to
get the widest possible circulation—the biggest audience.

Second, there is the man who keeps the paper or the station in business, who provides the profits—the advertiser. He may not want his name or his product to be advertised in a newspaper or on a station whose editorial views he does not agree with or which he feels might alienate his customers. By withholding the advertising dollar, he may exert influence.

Ours is a country of pressure groups—from the local parent-teacher association to powerful lobbies in Washington—and by means of everything from publicity handouts to the exertion of influence or implied threats of retribution, such groups may try to get material favorable to their interests into the news, and to suppress the unfavorable.

Freedom for the reporter to cover the news story—freedom of access, a vital press freedom—has been denied or curtailed in some instances since the beginning of news reporting, and today the fast media of radio and television are the cause of new ferment on the question of access. This has to do primarily with access to the activities of government, and applies to the executive branch, the legislative branch, and the courts, each of which has reasons to place restrictions of one kind or another on the journalist.

Curtailment of the paper's right to print and the broadcaster's right to air certain information prior to trial in criminal cases has been given the status of law by recent court decision, highlighting the knotty problem of how to allow a free press without denying any citizen a fair trial.

Last but not least of the forces that may plague any journalist in the course of doing his job is what is known as news management. By deliberately distorting or omitting some of what it makes available to the press and concurrently by controlling access of newsmen to its personnel, agencies of government or of private industry can shape a story to their liking. This is nothing new, but it is something today's reporter has to reckon with.

Another set of restrictions on the broadcast journalist's freedom belongs to him alone among journalists, and stems from the fact that all broadcasting operates under government regulation. To be in business, a broadcast station has to have a license from the federal government, which periodically must be renewed. His license can be removed for cause or a renewal denied. The regulatory agency for broadcasting is the FCC, which carries out this charge according to its own rules and the basic law adopted by Congress in 1934, the Federal Communications Act. There are certain regulations and policies of the Act and of the Commission which apply to the news and public affairs functions of the stations.

The first of these, which to be sure is not a restrictive burden for any responsible broadcaster, is a prohibition against the airing of obscenity.

The second—a requirement the reverse side of which is a restriction—is that broadcasters must operate in the "public interest, convenience and necessity." This is a spectacularly vague injunction, but as interpreted by the FCC it implies a reasonable amount of broadcast programming which offers the public informational or education services as opposed to pure entertainment. There is no doubt that whereas this requirement might be termed a restriction on the broadcaster, it is a positive stimulus to broadcast journalism.

However, the federal government does impose restrictions in some more specific ways. The first, in point of its seniority, is Section 315 of the Federal Communications

Act. This section requires that if a station gives airtime to a political candidate it must give equal time to all his opponents for the same office. This includes any and all splinter party candidates who may be on the ballot.

The other major restrictive area besides Section 315 is what is known as the Fairness Doctrine, which at present covers three subheadings. This doctrine is not part of the Federal Communications Act but emerged as an FCC rule-making action at the time (1949) the Commission decided to permit broadcast editorials. Basically, it states that if a station presents one side of a controversial issue, it must see that opportunity is provided for another side or sides of the issue to be aired. Two more rules are under consideration: If a licensee endorses a political candidate editorially, he must notify opposing candidates and offer reasonable opportunity for a candidate or his spokesman to respond within 24 hours of the airing of the editorial. The second, called the personal attack rule, is that a broadcaster must notify a person or group that has been attacked on his station, and must offer a "reasonable opportunity" to respond over the licensee's facilities.

Now let's take a look at how much these forces for restriction on the electronic newsman actually inhibit what he does. First, broadcast ownership.

At the national level, ownership or at least top management of the three networks have backed their news departments with ever-increasing financial support. They have entrusted the news job to competent professionals and left them alone to do a first-rate job in news programming. They have borne the costs for massive amounts of airtime devoted to live, special events. The network record on in-depth treatment of controversy is an uneven one, and critics see some softness here compared with the performance of several years ago. None of the networks editorializes, although this can be explained by considerations other than management timidity.

One factor which it seems big broadcast management takes into account these days is that its corporations are important listings on the Big Board in Wall Street. Veteran newsmen feel that power in the hands of profit-seeking stockholders makes for blander news policies than when "communicators" called the shots.

At the station level, management's commitment to journalism is easier to see. To oversimplify only slightly, the news director who is given a picayune budget—market size taken into consideration—little airtime, and no chance to report in depth or on controversial subjects, represents a boss who is playing it safe and handcuffing his newsmen. The boss of the station that does a lot with news, in-depth programming, and particularly editorializing, is plainly giving his news department a chance to do its job as it should be done. How much local management moves in to kill a news story or an idea for a controversial program is impossible for an outsider to know with certainty, but according to news directors of first-rate stations to whom I have talked, management takes the newsman's judgment, even if there are times when the newsman has to argue his case.

Electronic journalism seems to be completely free of any restrictions—save a minor one—that might be imposed on it by advertisers. Newsmen have been fiercely adamant about keeping advertisers out of their act, and management has backed them up. At both network and station level, sponsors are dropped before being allowed to have any say on what is broadcast in the name of news and public affairs. Here and there one could find exceptions, and one might well argue that the owner who minimizes news on his station might be the very one to bow to sponsor pressure, but for the most part broadcasting has a fine record on this score. One practice which alleviates possible trouble is that of permitting an advertiser freedom to remove his label from a program of controversy with which he may not want to be identified.

The one advertiser pressure that is bowed to by a substantial number of stations, though the networks have resisted it, is to permit the news announcer to deliver the commercial message. Good newsmen consider it out of place and of questionable integrity to ask the journalist to be a pitchman.

Only with the most pliable of managers do pressure groups have any influence in the news area. They cannot sway a news director unless they are clever enough to make him their unsuspecting cat's-paw.

Television is in a continuing battle to get access to the news for its cameras in some important areas where it is denied or circumscribed. Problems of this kind sometimes arise with the executive branches of government, though the trouble lies chiefly with the legislative and the judicial. For the executive, the President of the United States occupies, of course, a unique position as a subject for television attention and access. His every public move is fodder for television's cameras, and our television-age Presidents have all recognized the right of television to carry their speeches, their news conferences, their travels, their ceremonial appearances, their daily comings and goings to the viewers of the country.

Unlike other people, the President can command television airtime when he wants what he has to say to be broadcast. The networks are not bound by any law to provide him time, but in practice he nearly always gets live air, if not from all three networks then by one or two of them. The airtime he seeks is naturally a time that will assure him a substantial audience. Here and there presidential wishes concerning the use of television have been held by the networks to be discriminatory against their medium. Cameras are not always permitted to be present in the informal chats with men of the press sometimes called into President Johnson's White House office on short notice. There have been a few cases where presidential press secretaries have tried to set up separate news conferences with the President, one for the print medium and one for broadcasting. The networks protest such instances, insisting that whenever newsmen meet with the President, their cameras should have access. Occasionally a president has granted a request from one broadcaster without according equal access to other broadcasters, and this too has engendered complaints. In most cases, a network television interview with the Chief Executive will include a representative of each of the big three, so that equal treatment is observed. Generally, regular liaison between the broadcasting industry and the White House keeps presidential television relations on an even keel.

While the United States Congress has often been eager to have television look in on Congressional hearings and is not above using television as a platform, that body has steadfastly refused to allow television to cover Congress in session except on ceremonial occasions, such as the President's State of the Union Address. Broadcasters consider that being barred from the formal day-to-day proceedings of our highest legislative tribunal is a shocking restriction on their journalistic prerogatives.

Donald McGannon, President of Westinghouse Broadcasting Corporation, states the basic case for television's access to the Congress, state legislatures, and local governing bodies when he says:

Coverage of public events and activities particularly where they relate to those matters which are essential ingredients of our form of government and way of life, should be encouraged and extended to the maximum. In this manner we will achieve greater public understanding, awareness, interest, stimulation, response, and appreciation of these activities.[1]

To date, the Congress has not seen it this way. Our representatives seem to fear the all-seeing eye of television. But it is logical to assume that the camera's presence would bring about some changes in what takes place on the House and Senate floor, and that these changes, however agonizing to the lawmakers, would be for the betterment of the legislative process. At any rate, the television man argues that he has a right to take the story to the people with his tools, the microphone and camera, just as the newspaperman has the right to do with his tools, the pad and pencil.

Local and regional television have made inroads at the state level. Currently, forty state legislatures allow television to cover at least some of their sessions. It seems inevitable that in time the doors will be opened on Capitol Hill.

So far as the courts are concerned, the free-press versus fair-trial debate as it affects television camera access proceeds apace. Most states abide by Canon 35 of the American Bar Association, which excludes cameras and radio microphones, and supporters of this prohibition took additional heart when in 1965, by a five to four vote, the U. S. Supreme Court overthrew the conviction of Billie Sol Estes on the grounds that the presence of television in the Texas court that tried him denied the defendant a fair trial. Television men take issue with the thinking behind this decision and devoutly hope that the final word on the subject is yet to come. They consider denial of access to the courts to be a serious restriction on freedom of the press.

No responsible journalist wants the carrying out of his role to result in the denial of a fair trial to anyone, but the thoughtful and aroused men of television news make two points: Television coverage of a courtroom can be conducted with dignity and unobtrusiveness without disrupting the proceedings; and the American people have a right to know how their courts are being conducted, as a safeguard over one of the most vital parts of the democratic system, and television more than any other news medium is in a position to let them know.

One suspects that bar associations and judges are resisting this demand for television access for much the same reason as the U. S. Congress is—they simply prefer not to have everybody see what's going on. It may be a long fight and will take unceasing effort, but television will win eventually because of the reputation it is getting for being trustworthy and responsible as a news medium. In the world of the generation now growing up, television is not an alien presence on the scene of any part of our democratic process but a natural and necessary one. I submit that in a few years nothing will sound more dated than the words of Supreme Court Justice Tom Clark in the Estes decision: "A defendant on trial for a specific crime is entitled to his day in court, not in a stadium or a city or a nationwide arena. The heightened public clamor resulting from radio and television coverage will inevitably result in prejudice.

Trial by television is, therefore, foreign to our system."

Speaking for television when he was President of the Radio and Television News Directors' Association, Bruce Palmer provided an explanation for this kind of thinking:

The fact is that we may be hoist on our own petard; that is, many of the difficulties of access to information television news faces may be due to the amazing sophistication of communications of the last two decades. It is entirely possible that many elements of our society, such as the legal profession and the judges, the lawmakers and the law enforcement arms, have failed to keep pace in their thinking with the growth of television as a communications medium vital to the public.[2]

Pretrial publicity is another matter, and the mass media including television agree that here excesses are possible which may seriously jeopardize the rights of the accused. But they do not feel that denial of the right to print is an acceptable solution. Although television was a prominent communicator of information about Lee Harvey Oswald between the time of Kennedy's assassination and his own murder—some of which the Warren Report asserted might have rendered a fair trial impossible had he lived— any effort to bar television would have been considered by television men to be an intolerable restriction on them as journalists. The pretrial publicity question is in such a state of flux at this time that it is difficult to gauge what, if any, interdiction of news may eventuate.

Mass media watchdogs do not agree with some of the Warren Report conclusions. Particularly, they do not agree with those proposals resulting from the report from Congress, the courts, and the bar that would, if adopted, curb press freedom to cover and report as much of the story as it can get and as it feels it proper to publish. Admittedly, the record of American press, radio, and television has some black marks. The Sam Sheppard conviction for the murder of his wife in Cleveland was thrown out by the Supreme Court because the mass media had in effect tried Sheppard in the press. Radio and television interviews on the air with crime suspects immediately following their arrest raise serious questions about the chance of such suspects to have a fair trial. But the media feel that fettering newsmen by law as a remedy would only replace one evil with another.

A committee report of the American Society of Newspaper Editors best describes the case for press freedom. It said in part:

In many recent proposals by the bench and bar for corrective action, we feel that there has been a singular absence of recognition of the function the press in a democracy plays in serving the very ends that the bench and bar cherish: the proper administration of criminal justice.

If that part of the system (the political system in which many of our judges, prosecutors and sheriffs are elected officials) is to operate successfully, another part, the press, must exercise without fetters both its responsibility for watching the administration of justice and its freedom to report what it observes.

Reacting to the trend toward shutting off pretrial information from the time of an arrest until the beginning of a trial, the report said:

The democratic community is not only entitled to know promptly the facts about the crime and the progress of law enforcement and the administration of justice; democracy's successful functioning is endangered by lack of such knowledge.

To perform its functions the press must not be bound by the same regulations that govern the operation of the law enforcement agencies and the courts.[3]

In its conclusion, the committee recommended that the

press report criminal affairs, "with restraint, good taste and scrupulous regard for the rights of defendants, including the presumption of innocence, fair treatment and fair trial by unprejudiced jurors."

If radio, television, and newspaper reporters will follow such a course, then excesses likely to hurt a defendant will have to be laid at the door of the authorities—police spokesmen, judges, attorneys in the case. If controls are necessary it is on them that the controls should be placed, not on the people's eyes and ears—the journalists. Dean Erwin Griswold of Harvard Law School says:

If the lawyers will clarify the ground rules where lawyers and law enforcement officers are concerned, and will clearly publish these rules, most of the problems in the relations between the bar and the press will disappear—that persons accused of crime in this country will indeed have that "most basic right—a fair trial."[4]

What degree of restriction is imposed on the newsman by the management of news at its source? Able journalists who refuse to be cowed by frowning agencies of government are usually able to keep the effect of managed news within bounds. The best example of managed news in the mid-sixties is concerned with the Vietnam war. News policies of the Executive Branch of the Government have resulted in what is known as the "credibility gap" between the public and the White House. Here, through on-the-scene coverage abroad and coverage of the debate which has been going on at home, television has been a prime conveyor of the real picture, not the one the government would have us accept. News management at the community level is undergoing rough treatment at the hands of local stations' investigative reporters. Where newsmen exercise eternal vigilance, this will not be a serious problem.

When we come to government regulations which apply not to the print media or to the broadcast networks (which are not required to operate under federal government license) but to the 732 television stations of the country, the extent to which these regulations are considered impediments varies—as we have seen—from station to station. It is certain that some stations reduce or rule out their viewers' chances of seeing a candidate on free air time because of the obligations incurred through Section 315 of the Federal Communications Act. Likewise, the Fairness Doctrine requirement connected with the endorsement of a candidate discourages some stations from making any such endorsements. The personal attack rule and the Fairness Doctrine on balancing views on controversial issues are found by some fighting stations to be no deterrent, but have caused others to hesitate about or eschew altogether the broadcast editorial.

Just so long as men and organizations of the fourth estate tell the people what is going on in the world, just that long will there be forces at work to inhibit, restrict, or regulate the news. The ongoing struggle for the maintenance of the rights of the press is really one in which all media are involved and in which radio, television, and print should—must—act together. In most sectors of the fighting front the effort is a common effort. An exception is the government regulation reserved for broadcasting among the mass media, and here broadcasting has to fight alone.

The theory behind the laws that govern broadcasting is based on the idea that broadcasters use the public airwaves, which are limited in number, that therefore they are different from the publishers of newspapers, magazines, and books and must be regulated in the public interest. The broadcasting industry is girding for an all-out challenge to this idea, at least as it applies to broadcasting's role in journalism. It is basing its challenge on the U. S. Constitution itself, insisting that the constitutional protections of free press which cover print media are every bit as applicable to broadcasting. Action is planned in the courts—in the Supreme Court if necessary—to establish that constitutional protection is intended for the free dissemination of ideas irrespective of the method of communication.

The reasoning behind some of the restrictions imposed by the Federal Communications Act and the FCC is that since the frequencies on which broadcasting is transmitted are limited, there is danger of monopoly voices speaking in the community; the resulting insulation from any dissent or reply would constitute a denial to the people of access to many voices and many sides of questions. This reasoning has lost its validity according to the communications attorneys, who point out that today there are more broadcast stations in the United States than there are newspapers, that often it is the broadcaster who provides another voice in a newspaper monopoly town, and that with the opening up of additional frequencies in the broadcast band, no scarcity of channels for different views on the air actually exists.

Radio and television's contention is that Section 315 and the Fairness Doctrine in fact are unconstitutional, and that is what they hope the Supreme Court—which has never ruled on this issue—will decide if the case can be brought before it. In the meantime, the FCC will no doubt carry on in its present posture, that being, as the Commission sees it, its proper duty. Congress has shown little interest in making any changes. The courts are the only recourse for the broadcast journalist—a faintly ironic note in light of the confrontation between television and the judiciary on the matter of access.

The present governmental restrictions on the broadcaster may not be impossible for the television journalist to live with, but they are obnoxious as a matter of principle. As they encroach on electronic journalism they are a hindrance to press freedom, and as such they must be attacked. It would be well for all press freedoms if the print journalist made this issue—his broadcast brethren's fight—his own.

TWELVE

THE MEN
OF ELECTRONIC
JOURNALISM

Within a medium whose most profitable business is mass
entertainment, the television journalist has had to fight
his way to the position he now occupies, where he and his
place on the air have to be taken seriously. He works cheek
by jowl with personnel on the same payroll whose preoccupation is purely show business, with the trivia and
mediocrity which often accompany it when the objective
is to reach the widest possible audience. Broadcast news
has kept from being engulfed in this bottomless pit and
has created what that outspoken critic of low quality
television, former FCC Chairman Newton Minow, would
call "an oasis in the vast wasteland." That it has done this
must be credited to the dedication, the enterprise, and the
integrity of those men who see the opportunity and the
responsibility of television as a medium of journalism.

Network and station managers who stand by convictions
of their own or are willing to be convinced by others, have
to be given initial credit. Newsmen who as administrators,
editors, and news directors, build the news organization

and lead the drive for budget, for airtime, for tools to do a competent job, furnish the heart of the achievement. Reporters, anchormen, leg men, who are the communicators with the viewer of the news program, give the stamp of authority to the whole enterprise. And the young army of unseen specialists—the cameraman, the film editor, the writer, the editorial editor, the documentarian—make the television journalist the master of his at once highly effective and terribly complicated medium of communication.

It is unlikely that one could find, in any of the many areas devoted to the gathering and dissemination of news, as wide a variety of people in type and background as is found in television journalism. They come from newspapers, wire services, news magazines, radio, television, film, and photography. For example, Jim Bennett, who runs a news organization with a commendable record at KLZ in Denver, began his career as a photographer; he learned the news side as he went along. Others come from academia, from electronic engineering, from show business. Some started as journalists and learned television; some, as broadcasters who learned news. Wherever they came from and whatever kinds of people they are, they are developing through their common absorption in television journalism a new breed, sired by the demands of the medium.

And their medium is the most demanding of them all. To all the capabilities and standards of good journalism, the television man must add a thorough understanding of how to use the prime tools of his medium—the pictorial elements; the oral word as distinct from the printed word; the unique status of a camera and an air reporter each of which becomes part of the news report; and the combining of everything into a presentation which is more than the sum total of the parts because the blending of the ingredients adds something intangible that wasn't there before.

Today's men of television news are the beneficiaries of the pioneering efforts of earlier men in the field, a few of whom, like Frank Stanton of CBS, have positions at the top of the industry today. Men like Paul White of CBS and Abe Schechter of NBC set earlier news standards for radio which were successfully transferred to the sight medium. Gilbert Seldes, Frank McCall, and others were among the small band of men who strove to apply television's tools to news in the days before and just after World War II. Ed Murrow and Fred Friendly pioneered new methods for television journalism and set a standard for courage and integrity which still serves as a model for the newsmen in the field. As President of NBC, Robert Kintner helped his men build a television news organization second to none, and sparked a lively period of growth in news departments everywhere.

Through the years the networks gathered to their news organizations an extraordinary group of reporters, who represent the visible link between those organizations and the people of the country. David Brinkley, Charles Collingwood, Walter Cronkite, Chet Huntley, William H. Lawrence, Edward P. Morgan, Merrill Mueller, John Scali, Daniel P. Schorr, Eric Sevareid, Howard K. Smith, Robert Trout—reporters such as these not only provide the personality and tone as front men, but their journalistic know-how and integrity have helped make their organizations the responsible entities they are.

A turn toward the specialized journalist in broadcasting was made by ABC in 1960, when that company appointed Jules Bergman the first network science editor. The superiority of this science-trained broadcaster over nonspecialists, however capable, has been particularly evident in television's coverage of the space story and confirms the soundness of the specialization idea.

We have noted earlier how the building up and filling out of their journalistic functions by the networks stimulated the same progress in the development of news departments and responsibilities by the stations. Just as the caliber of the product nationally reflects the caliber of the network newsmen, so does the caliber of the best local product reflect the qualities of station men.

As there had to be farsighted and public spirited management people like Frank Stanton, Bob Kintner, and Leonard Goldenson at the network level, their equivalents at the community level also had to be receptive to the idea of giving news its proper place. In some part led by the managers of network owned and operated stations and spurred on by their network bosses, affiliates and independents of several shapes and sizes came up with friends of news in the ranks of management and ownership. Manager Robert Wood of KNXT and Clark George of WCBS-TV support and take a lively interest in their news departments. Every one of Time-Life Broadcasting's five television station managers is a champion of news. Likewise with Westinghouse Broadcasting Corporation. May Broadcasting Corporation owns KMTV, Omaha, and backs its newsmen all the way; so do the Kelly Brothers, owners of KCRA, Sacramento; and the Bullitt family which owns the KING stations in the Pacific Northwest; and the Stern family which owns WDSU in New Orleans. The owner-manager of WBOX in Bogalusa was forced out of business by his responsible journalism.

In the sixties, as the counterparts of Bill McAndrew, Fred Friendly, and Elmer Lower, three outstanding network news chiefs, there is a remarkable group of young station news directors who perhaps more than anybody else personify the new breed.

Robert Gamble, News Manager of WFBM, Indianapolis, and in 1966 President of the Radio-TV News Directors Association, runs an aggressive shop for his news oriented manager, Eldon Campbell. With the staff of capable newsmen he has gathered around him, Bob goes in for responsible prodding in his community that has earned the station a reputation as a constructive journalistic force.

Eddie Barker, KRLD, Dallas, has built a news organization (now housed in perhaps the finest physical plant of any television newsroom in the country) that provides its community with a first rank news service and is not afraid to take on the Dallas oligarchy when occasion demands.

Young veteran news directors Dick Cheverton (Grand Rapids), John Corporon (New Orleans), Bill McGivern (St. Paul) and Steve Fentress (St. Louis) have all done the painstaking job of building a staff, gained the confidence of the community (officialdom and the public alike) and constantly raised their sights on their news performance in ways that account for the viewers' growing dependence on television journalism.

There are promising news directors in their twenties and early thirties who are beginning to set a fast pace in this young man's game. Mark Gautier of Omaha, Bob McBride and Bill Fyffe, both of Detroit, Dick Goldberg of Chicago, and Joe Bartelme of Minneapolis display the thoughtfulness of mature news executives while retaining the youthful enthusiasm of cub reporters. As one of them describes his operation, "We're Bill Hearst with responsibility."

What spurs on men like this to work as hard as they do,

to confront frightening responsibility, to fight for budgets, to be on call twenty-four hours a day like a doctor, to stay on year after year at the same station, is explained by one of the young veterans who has been doing just these things for nearly twenty years at WTVJ in Miami, Ralph Renick.

News . . . is the reason for local stations existing. News is the only vestige of creative local programming left. . . . News is the only point adequately differentiating between a good station and a bad station. News is the barometer used to determine if a station is fulfilling its so-called public service obligation to the community it serves and the barometer which dictates whether an FCC license should be pasted back on the wall for another three year hitch. News is the main identifying watermark of a station. News is the only means of separating the men from the boys. News means us. We are the men who run these shops and who supervise the men who program these millions of hours of information put forth over the air each month. So it's no wonder we don't have a great turnover in our ranks. The job is just too important and challenging. For most of us, the opportunity to create, to see ideas reach fruition, to see a town bettered—all of this gives us the satisfaction.[1]

Renick is not only a news executive; he is also a Miami celebrity by virtue of his regular air appearances. Television airmen also are a part of the new breed. Men such as Cronkite, Huntley, Brinkley, and Jennings are hardly more well known in their sphere than are the local broadcast men in theirs.

The member of the new breed who is seen on the air every day is described by one news director I talked to simply as "a reporter and writer who sounds good and looks good." There is a temptation to surround the question of what qualities make a newsman successful on the air with a mystique that my informant resisted in the above definition. But I think the intangible qualities less cautious students of this phenomenon would ascribe to the successful air reporter can be described in one word: believability. He must have that if all the effort, ingenuity, and high standards employed by the best of news teams are to make their impact on the viewing public. Some may decry the star system, but it is inevitable in a medium of such personal character, which in turn is one of its great strengths. The man who has this special chemistry, be he a trained newsman or a magnetic personality, will be found at the post of anchorman, star field reporter, documentary narrator, or air editorialist in every successful television station news operation in the country. A station that has the town's favorite newsman can beat a rival station however good the rival's news product may be.

John Griffin at WTAR, Norfolk, is one of that kind; so is Jerry Dunphy at KNXT, Los Angeles, and Howard Caldwell at WFBM, Indianapolis. Bill Beutel of WABC-TV, New York, evokes belief among his audience; so do Eddie Barker in Dallas and John Facenda in Philadelphia.

Older men like Len O'Connor in Chicago have a large and loyal following. So do young men like Mel Dominic at WKY, Oklahoma City, and John Palmer at WMAQ, Chicago. Cool, studious-looking Ray Moore is "big" in Atlanta; informal, folksy Baxter Ward in Los Angeles and sober Ray Miller in Houston have a similar stature.

Newswomen on the air have gained only a slim beachhead at the networks, but they are well established on local broadcasts. Wanda Ramey, KPIX in San Francisco, and Liz Trotta, WNBC, New York, are examples. In many a three-station town, such as Sacramento, all the stations have women on their television air. And they are not just doing the weather or the women's page. They are general assignment reporters. Some, like Miss Ramey, a political reporter, are specialists. This is a significant breakthrough, and judging from performances to date, newswomen are proving their capability and we shall be seeing more of them.

Many station newsmen are good, but there are not yet enough of them to go around. Stations raid each other for top talent, and the networks raid the stations—a sign that promising material is developing out there in the communities. NBC's Frank McGee was called to the big time from Oklahoma; ABC's Frank Reynolds from Chicago; NBC's Alex Gifford from New Orleans and Tom Pettit from Iowa; CBS's Eric Sevareid from Minneapolis and Charles Kuralt from North Carolina.

The air reporters constitute the glamorous contingent of the new breed. And glamour is a necessary part of all television. But at good stations it is not allowed to get in the way of the serious business of the news, and of the responsibility attached to it. It is in the area of responsibility that the new breed is proving that it is worthwhile and that it merits respect.

"Don't take anybody else's word for it" is an axiom of the careful journalist. Unfortunately, it was not always put into practice in the broadcast newsroom, where practically all the news was gathered by nonbroadcast sources. Today, whether the source is a newspaper, one of the wire services, or the broadcaster's own staff, checking the story for accuracy is the rule of good news directors.

When you are researching a story for a news program or an in-depth treatment, or gathering facts for an editorial, you don't—if integrity is your copilot—predetermine what you'll come out with. You let your evidence decide. Broadcast newsmen have learned to accept this kind of journalistic discipline.

"Tabloid [sensational] journalism is not a service to the community," says Jon Poston, News Director, Sioux City, and the choice of stories on the news programs of responsible television stations reflects commendable resistance to tabloidism. Enlightened management and the news executive in charge constantly seek avenues of journalistic endeavor which will be of constructive service to their communities. Ray Moore in Atlanta carried out, through WSB News, a thoughtfully prepared campaign to help the people of his city to understand the good sense of complying with antisegregation laws, so that Atlanta would avoid the searing explosion that struck some southern areas. In order to forestall such trouble in a community which would be all too likely to say, "It can't happen here," Deacon Anderson, in Seattle, is doing an educational job on KING while time remains to do it. Ed Barker, who is not above stirring things up in Dallas, shows another side of the responsible news director's concern. He holds that while going all-out when the situation demands it, the news director must consider the position of station ownership and of legitimate power centers in the community as a whole, and should use his powerful medium and the freedoms vested in him with restraint.

I have talked at length and many times with a number of the leaders of the new breed, and find that they indulge in much soul searching about the powerful journalistic tool they control. They carry under the surface more humility than could have been found in the character of newsmen of an older generation. They say again and again that they must find better ways to do a better job as journalists. They are nagged and spurred on by the knowledge that people are depending on television, and they are keenly aware that that segment of the viewers which depends on them the most is turning virtually nowhere else for what it must learn about what is going on in the world.

When a part of the world or the community is in flames, the sense of responsibility of today's broadcast journalist is manifest most dramatically. I will not soon forget the graphic film closeup I saw in the screening room of a station in Detroit—vignette of violence during a race riot —which showed a Negro policeman smashing his fist into the face of his white superior. For graphic impact it was all a television newsman could want. The news director's sense of responsibility prevailed; the film was never shown on the air.

The violent four days in Watts in the summer of 1965 put the fast media under great strain. The difficulties of covering the running story with microphone and camera, and the physical danger to the newsmen themselves, were compounded by anguishing questions as to what to shoot and edit and say, and whether or not to release the story. Keep the public informed, yes, but what about contributing to or prolonging the disturbance? There were excesses committed by non-newsmen from non-news stations, but in the main there was sane conduct. In the heat of things, the best of the broadcast men could still think about their responsibilities and try to live up to a higher ethic than simply getting the sensational story and dispensing it.

When the city of Omaha was reported to be in for a Watts-type uprising over Labor Day weekend in 1965, I saw on the bulletin board in the newsroom of KMTV a memorandum to all hands. To me, it so typifies the spirit of responsibility of the new breed that I take the liberty of reprinting it here in full:[2]

SUBJ: Reporting of possible racial disturbances

1. There are hundreds of rumors circulating concerning possible racial violence on the Near Northside during the Labor Day week-end. Law enforcement officials are concerned and are taking precautions to have all possible manpower available if needed.

2. The Public Safety Director and Police Chief say they do NOT plan to have a multitude of officers or cruisers swarming in on every "drunk," "disturbance," "loitering," or "fighting" call. They plan to police such calls as usual, make arrests as quietly as possible, and get out as quickly as possible. They suggest that it would be possibly detrimental if a number of newsmen made an appearance on such routine calls in anticipation that the "lid might blow." They request that we be extremely careful in this respect. Their request is reasonable and presents little problem since we normally do not cover such calls anyway.

3. We have been assured that, should violence erupt, there will be adequate radio traffic to alert us to that fact. From that point on, we must exercise responsible judgment. Here are some specific guidelines:

   a. We will *not* bulletin information concerning racial disturbances in progress unless it becomes apparent that we must do so to serve the best public interest. This is a judgment call, and a tough one, but every care must be taken to avoid attracting crowds into troubled areas or to in any way impede police efforts to control the situation.

   b. We will cooperate with authorities in every way. We will report factually and in as non-inflammatory a manner as possible on our regularly scheduled newscasts.

   c. Care must be exercised in wording of copy. The term "riot" will be avoided unless the facts are indisputable. And remember . . . a riot is not necessarily a "race riot." A "race-riot" involves fighting between large numbers of white and non-white citizens. When the conflict involves citizens and law officers, no matter what color, the term "race riot" is highly questionable.

d. Charges of "police brutality" must be investigated carefully and not aired indiscriminately. Should such charges be made, we must make every effort to establish the facts leading up to the alleged incident or incidents. Police Command Officers should be sought out for comment. The use of violence to combat violence certainly doesn't constitute "police brutality." Be careful of that trap.

e. The Police chain-of-command for information is as follows: Public Safety Director Lynch, Chief Smith, and Inspector Al Pattavina. Every effort should be made to verify reports with responsible officials. It has always been our policy NOT to report rumors involving the health, safety or welfare of the public, and a period of racial tension is certainly no excuse for relaxing this policy.

f. It is impossible to anticipate what situations may occur, but I know you will continue to demonstrate responsible reporting as you have done in the past.

Mark Gautier, *News Director*

At the time this book is written, the story of broadcasting's new breed would not be complete without a word of tribute for its most valiant members—the war correspondents in Vietnam. On July 12, 1966, NBC News correspondent Ron Nessen was wounded by enemy fire while covering a search action of the 101st Airborne Division in the Central Highlands. What NBC cameraman Peter Boultwood, who was with Nessen, reported back home says best what can be said of all his kind:

As a team we have had more close calls in the past few months than we care to think about, but Ron Nessen never took foolish risks. He often admitted that he was scared, as we all are under fire. But he took the risks necessary to cover the war the way he felt it should be covered—from the front lines with the troops. As a close friend and cameraman, I could never wish to work with a braver and more dedicated correspondent.[3]

THIRTEEN

WHAT'S AHEAD
IN ELECTRONIC
JOURNALISM

Before discussing the future of electronic journalism, it is necessary to take notice of those areas in which there is room for improvement, in other words, the shortcomings of electronic journalism. It is essential to do this in any case, to reply to those readers who are saying that in most of the foregoing I have been biased on the side of the broadcaster and have painted him as a white knight, above reproach in his devotion to the highest tenets of news responsibility, when there is evidence to the contrary.

Of course, there are shortcomings in both the network and the station news situations. In the area of live coverage of special events, for instance, the three networks—for competitive or other reasons—practice an all-or-nothing policy which results in over-coverage (by all three), or abbreviated or no coverage. Why can't they divide the job for any given occasion and give the public more total coverage, at the same time providing viewers with a choice of parallel programs of entertainment?

Network regular news programs, while difficult to find

fault with, do leave some things to be desired. They should provide more commentary by men now on their staffs who are capable of it. On Vietnam alone, as Jack Gould says:

For television itself, the deluge of conflicting information on the ramifications of the Vietnamese conflict suggests a clear urgency for much more interpretive commentary than is now being offered. . . . A balanced presentation of official pros and cons by Administration and Congressional representatives is not enough; the viewer deserves an assessment by the journalists, following the precedent set by such giants of yester-year as Bill Shirer, Elmer Davis, Ed Murrow and Raymond Swing. When a country's chips are on the table, the viewing public will sit still for illuminating commentary.[1]

Recently there has been an alarming proliferation of commercial messages on some network and some station news programs. The number of advertisements and amount of airtime involved exceed the recommendations of the broadcasters themselves through the NAB code. And they invite backlash from viewers.

The networks have not made a big or consistent enough effort in the field of investigative reporting, and could take a leaf from the book of some aggressive local stations in this regard. And they need to find a better answer to the admittedly tough problem of freeing their airmen for first-hand coverage of the news they report. Messrs. Cronkite and Brinkley and their counterparts are not as free as they should be to spend the time they should on the personal research and reporting needed to keep up with the news and the meaning of the news, particularly when they know that their glamorous position causes audiences to accept what they say without any kind of critical attitude.

The networks do not tackle as many controversial subjects as it is necessary to put before their viewers, and part of the time at least they treat controversy with a kind of artificial balancing of views which can amount to distortion. Occasionally too, in documentary and other in-depth programs, sponsors of the program or elements of our society being examined in the program are given favored treatment, to the detriment of objective journalism.

Editorializing is a vital journalistic force in a democracy, and our national radio and television industry defaults in a great potential service in this respect, even though networks face very substantial problems in such an effort. At least one of them ought to try the idea, mentioned most recently by Columbia Journalism Professor Fred Friendly, of leaving time at the close of a network show on a public issue for each station carrying the program to append its own view in the form of an editorial.

Some critics try to use the numbers game to demonstrate how the networks are producing fewer public affairs programs this year than last, but I think this is a rather meaningless exercise. They do have a point in the matter of the broadcast hours chosen for the airing of such programs. Inter-network competition for audiences, sponsor considerations, and therefore dollars and cents are involved, and these cannot be passed off lightly; but it is certainly true that many fine informational programs are given ghetto air time, and many possible viewers never see them.

When we come to criticism that must in conscience be made of television stations and their jobs in news, we find one big, overriding fault, and that is that too many of them don't do the job. The stations referred to in this book represent the best of the lot, and the best stations probably add up to less than half of the 616 commercial television stations in the fifty states and the District of Columbia.

Of the rest, some do a part of the job they should, some are going to do it, they say, at some future time, and some are clearly going to skip the responsibility altogether if they can get away with it. This is the most discouraging aspect of the entire television news picture today—the absence of any real news responsibility on the part of some station operators.

The situation has not been helped by those timorous or dollar-conscious managers who get only their toes wet by giving news a try with prohibitively small budgets and staffs, or who will not stay with the effort for the requisite amount of time. A successful television news operation is not created overnight. Such people do not give it a chance. Insisting that the news department pay its way is not discharging the responsibility, though a good many do pay their way. Periodic management economy waves have hurt some station news operations badly, as there is rarely any cushion to absorb the blow.

Two shortcomings found in some otherwise excellent (larger market) news operations are related to how much the news director is allowed to spend. One is the absence of facilities to cover the state capital when it is a city other than that of the station, though this is the station's most important regional news source. The other is the lack of specialist reporters needed to give expert coverage to political, economic, scientific, and educational fields as vital today at the local as at the national and international level.

Not all the good news stations are lily white in their allocations of airtime for special programs any more than the networks are, and otherwise top performers put up some fine-sounding arguments on why 11:30 on Saturday mornings is such advantageous airtime for a public affairs program. A more serious charge can be made against many network affiliated stations for their failure to carry important depth treatment programs offered to them by their networks. Some vital public issue—often one the local station cannot or will not itself deal with—is lost entirely to its viewers.

It must be admitted that the matter of assigning good airtime to public service, which usually means the pre-empting of an entertainment program, is complicated by the attitude of the very person the broadcaster is trying to serve—the viewer. A highly vocal minority of Americans resent the interruption of their nightly opiate for any reason whatever, and are quick to register their resentment. The performance of some of our citizens in protesting loudly when Batman was canceled because two of our astronauts were in serious trouble in space in March of 1966 was nothing short of monstrous. One can only hope that broadcasters will have skins thick enough to allow them to ignore such people.

There are two other station shortcomings that deserve mention. Some stations that do a fine job on hard news rarely if ever get into controversial matters, though their communities may have a crying need for at least the airing and interpretation of a local issue if not a point of view from the station. And second, among the growing number of stations that editorialize, almost none tackles national or international issues. In the absence of network editorializing, this leaves a yawning gap unfilled.

Television could do better by electronic journalism than it is yet doing, and thus more for the people of America. What are the people of America to expect in ten or fifteen years from this medium, which they have already honored with a high vote of confidence? First, let's see what the

157

scientist and the electronic engineer are preparing in the way of tools to do the job with.

As this is written, they have already launched into an era of technological capacity which was only in the testing laboratory just a few years ago. Studio film and videotape color are here, and their use is spreading rapidly. Network-station and interstation closed circuit systems are used for instant airing or recording of live, film, and tape material throughout most of the country. Still pictures and copy go the same route by facsimile transmission. Quicker editing, and incredible things like stopping the action of a story at will, are making videotape—one of the greatest of all inventions for television—into an even more versatile tool.

Miniaturizing has been so perfected that high fidelity cameras and sound equipment can both be carried by one man at the scene of the news. The television newsman can go places he could not get into with his bulkier gear. He can come closer than ever to bringing every nuance of the sight and sound of the story to his viewers. And he can do it in a completely unobtrusive manner. In making some of these advances, the engineer has brought new opportunities to more telecasters than ever, because costs of operation are being reduced to the point where they are within the capacity of the smaller station budget.

The sending of live pictures from space is a reality with heady ramifications. So, of course, is the orbiting communications satellite, whose vast potential for television we have only begun to tap.

Continuous refinements lie ahead in all the tools we have now. And the use of the most exciting of them will be expanded as fast as the budgets and the imaginations of the telecasters can catch up with what the scientist and engineers have wrought. All of us will be aboard vicariously when our astronauts reach the moon and beyond. Communications satellites will provide us with myriad visual and sound links, of which instant worldwide television and instant relay services with a nearly infinite number of channels within the United States are only the beginning. On this score, Joseph V. Charyk, President of the Communications Satellite Corporation, predicts an "information revolution that will recast the nature of the world in which we live." He speaks of a communications utility to be established in metropolitan centers, and says:

This would be a system which would link homes, business offices and stores in a community through transmission facilities to central switching and computing centers to provide a wide variety of services. This would include color television and stereophonic FM radio, aural and visual telephonic service, high-speed facsimile data and newspapers, library reference, theater and transportation booking services, access to computer facilities, shopping and banking services of all kinds, centralized charging and billing. . . . Communications destined beyond this metropolitan area would be directed to a processing and transmission center which, in turn, would be linked through a suitable terminal station to a world wide satellite system.[2]

The application of all the new tools by television journalists may make its own revolution in the field of news and news dissemination. Instead of being a news medium which works alongside others, it may in time play a role at the heart of the gathering and reporting of all news, whether it is print or voice and picture news. The tremendous electronic hardware it will have to command for its own purposes argues that these facilities might be put to work to do the job of local, national, and worldwide news gathering now performed by the wire services like AP and

UPI. It might become the transmitter of today's newspaper—instantly and in color into its viewers' homes.

It will certainly combine its new capacity to cover the world live with its already established capacity to capitalize on the fabulous data computer, to expand the instant poll (with the help of instant language translators) into an international vehicle. It goes without saying that the face-to-face dialogue among world leaders which is already feasible will soon be possible on a world scale, and the opportunities if offers for peace and understanding among nations can hardly be ignored in the years ahead by those men in power who hold the fate of humanity in their hands.

The future of television will be a future which includes more informational programming from a steadily increasing number of television sources, from the present three national networks plus a fourth commercial network now in the planning stage, from the present commercial television stations plus new ones in the UHF band, from educational television, and very possibly from Community Antenna Television (CATV) and pay television.

Fred Friendly foresees that some time in the 1970s more than half of network prime night time will be devoted to informational programming of one kind or another. Whether or not this happens, there are going to be more network and station news time, more budget allocations, larger and more professional news staffs. It follows that the greater amount of television news will offer solid content more imaginatively produced than it is today, with the result that its audiences will be as big as if not bigger than they are today.

The all-channel television receiver, soon to be universal, makes UHF (channel numbers 14 to 83) available to all viewers and will speed the proliferation of stations, impeded until now by the scarcity of channels in the VHF band (2 to 13) of the spectrum. This is particularly important in areas of the country which up to this time have had only one or two stations to tune to, but it will mean additional stations in every place that can economically support more than they have now. This is likely to open up new avenues for news, information, and public affairs, for the viability of some of the new stations will depend on their providing something different. That "something" may be specialization in news—as some radio stations are already doing—or providing information and educational programming in subject fields now given short shrift by conventional commercial stations.

Educational television, which has the potential for making substantial contributions in electronic journalism, has recently attracted a kind of high-level support which may lead to endowing it with a secure and more productive future. In the summer of 1966, the Ford Foundation proposed what Jack Gould of the *New York Times* calls "an exciting, visionary concept of a satellite television system that would channel commercial TV expenditures into the support of noncommercial [i.e., educational] television." [3] Essentially, the idea is that if the money which networks now spend for cable and microwave to send programs across the country were used to provide the same service by orbiting satellites, millions of dollars would be saved, some of which could be used to support educational television. There would be room on the satellites to transmit educational programs free, thereby making possible an educational network of the (currently) 130 educational stations in the country.

Later, Ford unveiled a 10-million-dollar project to provide educational television with a three-hour demonstration program every Sunday night, which would tap the men and resources of our great universities to illuminate a broad spectrum of subject matter of concern to thinking Americans.

In January, 1967, a commission financed by the Carnegie Corporation—the Carnegie Commission on Educational Television—issued its report, two years in the making, setting forth its ideas for permanent solutions to educational television's programs. The report recommended the establishment of a nongovernment, nonprofit Corporation for Public Television which would expand the program distribution to educational stations now provided by National Educational Television, encourage production by leading stations for distribution to the rest, link up stations to permit simultaneous transmission nationally, and make grants of funds to stations commensurate with their needs to develop and improve local programming. Financing of these activities would be provided through a federal manufacturer's excise tax on television sets at the time they are sold to the public. President Johnson in a message to the Congress (February 28th) urged the creation of such a Corporation for Public Television, initially financed from federal funds. It seems likely, therefore, that some significant action to strengthen and enhance the role of educational television and its journalistic contribution will not be long in coming.

CATV has newly become a controversial element in the television world, and the shape of its future is uncertain. It is at least going to make more of the existing television programs available to more viewers, even if it doesn't become a news source per se. This technical system, basically designed to pick television signals off the air by means of a master antenna and then pipe them into homes where reception is poor, has gone beyond its original uses —welcomed by broadcast stations—and now offers additional services (made possible by multi-channel equipment) which could put CATV into competition with stations. This development has the industry up in arms. The FCC now recognizes CATV as coming within its jurisdiction, and at this writing it remains to be seen how its role will be defined by the government regulators.

Another form of television that has undergone a trial period in a few picked communities is pay television through which programs not available on regular television could be seen by home owners willing to pay a per-program or a monthly fee for the privilege. If this form takes hold, and if it comes under the same regulation as the free television stations, then its segment of programming in the "public interest convenience and necessity" will certainly include informational if not news material.

We are going to have more of everything—more and better tools, more news, more sources, more audience— but there is still a larger question that will finally determine whether electronic journalism lives up to its potential and to its challenge. As John Schneider, President of the CBS Broadcasting Group, says: "Certainly in ten years, we will have an instant communications capability, world wide. But as to what we are going to say to the world when we have their attention, I'm not certain yet." [4] Mr. Schneider may be assailed by the same doubts that impelled British science writer Arthur C. Clarke to express the fear that we are creating a communications capability that is so sophisticated that it will outstrip the capacity of man's brain. There may come a time, he concludes wryly, when only machines can talk to machines. On that unhappy day we shall have no choice but to "tiptoe away and leave them to it."

We must reject that chilling thought. We must talk, but what we say is the crux of the whole affair. No one has to be a seer to predict that our complex, nuclear-age world and the problems of human society are going to get more complicated rather than less, and that tomorrow's citizens of a democracy must be wiser than their grandfathers if we are to survive and build a better world. Walter Lippmann, James Reston, Eric Sevareid, all have warned that the burden is on the journalist to exert leadership in preparing the people for what they have to face, to bring them not only information but also enlightenment. Television cannot escape a vital role in this endeavor.

What must lie ahead for television news is to uncover, realistically and fearlessly, the basic truths of our times. It must tackle the really important news, the important problems, the controversial questions, and speak out editorially with candor and integrity. Even if television journalism does not in time become the only medium for reaching the many segments of the American public, it will be the prime source for most of us. Hayakawa has stated, about television: "Already it has brought the whole big startling world into the lives and imagination of millions who would never have been able to discover it through reading." As the poor man's newspaper, television has a special educational responsibility to act as a sophisticating agency in the best sense of that term. I think electronic journalism will live up to the challenge of journalistic leadership, simply because it is too great and important a medium to do less. If television does less, Ed

Murrow said only a few years ago, "Surely we shall pay for using this most powerful instrument of communication to insulate the citizenry from the hard and demanding realities which must be faced if we are to survive."

A. William Bluem, in his book called the *Documentary in American Television*, said something about documentaries which I think applies to all electronic journalism as we look ahead:

The possibilities are all but overwhelming. If we possess the technology by which to obliterate ourselves, we also have the capacities to harness technology in the responsible service of mankind—seeking not only an essential betterment and a new level of harmony among men and nations, but the individualization of man. Even the most skeptical detractors of the mass media will admit that television, in its greatest moments, has served both goals. For all can sense that the images on the TV screen help to create, for the first time in human history, *communicating man*—a creation which underlies both a social and an individual view of life.[5]

Between now and the year 2,000, when the population of our country will be more than 250 million, the scope, the acceptance, and the responsibilities of television journalism will grow and continue to grow. My own evaluation is that the leadership in the field, the men who count and the men who will count a few years from now, are humbly aware of the magnitude of that responsibility and are already on the move to meet it. The strengths of television journalism well outweigh its weaknesses as of now, and the faith and dependence a great many viewers are placing in it will be rewarded in times to come. I predict a proud future for the journalist whose medium has made communicating man possible.

In my travels around the country to do research for this book I found—and I think it must have come through plainly to the reader—the greatest vitality today to be at the station level of television news. My new colleague on the faculty at the Graduate School of Journalism at Columbia University, Fred Friendly, seems to be similarly persuaded. He recently said to me, "The next Edward R. Murrow will come from a station." And that, from Ed's longtime friend and admirer, translates into the ultimate salute.

The rousing spirit that echoes from the hustings is put into words by the General Manager of station WOOD-TV in Grand Rapids, Willard Schroeder:

Those who run commercial television boast of a well earned reputation for sensing what the audience wants and giving it to them. As a group, I think they're a pretty perceptive bunch— and they are realists. They realize that there really are thought leaders in our society, and that this isn't just a threadbare term for a certain variety of egghead. What these people, the genuine thought leaders, think and do is a fairly reliable indication of what we can expect from some of the lower echelons before long.

That's why I think, those of us in commercial television are tooling up for information programming, why we are beginning to put news men into top level executive jobs, why we are running longer news programs, more documentaries, covering more events on location. More and more of our audience want us to be where the action is, to communicate to them the sight and sound of what's going on. We don't intend to disappoint them.[6]

For many people, television is going to be the prime source of knowledge of the contemporary world. For the sake of these people alone, television is faced with shouldering a larger share of the mass media load than radio, newspapers, and periodicals. It is a tremendous challenge. It is fervently to be hoped that there will be enough Willard Schroeders, Howard Smiths, Frank Stantons, and Mark Gautiers coming along to meet that challenge with courage and persistence.

NOTES

Chapter *1*. Television—Indispensable Medium for News
1. Elmo Roper and Associates, *The Public's View of Television and Other Media, 1959–1964*. Issued March 15, 1965.
2. John H. Murphy, Address, National Newspaper Promotion Association, Atlanta, Georgia, as reported in *Editor & Publisher*, May 1, 1965, page 64.

Chapter *3*. News as It Is Happening
1. Theodore H. White, *The Making of the President, 1964*, Atheneum, 1965, page 233.

Chapter *5*. In-Depth Programs
1. Dr. Frank Stanton, Address to Canadian Broadcast Executives Society, Montreal, March 23, 1966.
2. A. William Bluem, *The Documentary in American Television.* Hastings House, 1965, page 109.

Chapter *7*. Commentary, Controversy, and Persuasion
1. Harry Reasoner, "Problems of Reporting Controversial Issues," Address to New York Chapter, American Council for

Judaism, via leased wire from radio station KMOX, St. Louis, February, 1966.

2. Group W Release, February 10, 1965.

3. This statement was made to the author by letter.

4. John Dille, "Democracy and Media Interaction," *Television Quarterly*, Winter 1965, p. 36.

5. Norman Swallow, "Instant Truth," article in *Contrast*, Summer 1963. Published by British Film Institute, London.

Chapter 8. Television as a Maker of News

1. John Dunne, "TV's Riot Squad," *News Republic*, September 11, 1965, page 27.

2. Theodore H. White, *The Making of the President, 1960*, Atheneum, 1961, page 190.

3. *Newsweek Magazine*, June 30, 1966, page 84.

Chapter 9. A Case History—Civil Rights and Television

1. William Monroe, "The Racial Crisis and the News Media," remarks at a meeting sponsored by ADL and the Freedom of Information Center, University of Missouri, November 16, 1965.

2. *Ibid.*

3. S. I. Hayakawa, "Television and the Negro Revolt," *Television Quarterly*, Summer 1964, pages 24 and 25.

4. Eric Sevareid to the author.

5. Joseph Brechner, "The Racial Crisis and the News Media," remarks at a meeting sponsored by ADL and the Freedom of Information Center, University of Missouri, November 16, 1965.

Chapter 11. Forces Which Inhibit Broadcast Journalism

1. Donald H. McGannon, "Fair Trial versus a Free Press," an occasional paper on the Free Society, published by the Center for the Study of Democratic Institutions, 1965, page 30.

2. Bruce Palmer, "What Is the Future for Television News?" *Television Age*, October 11, 1965, page 74.

3. Report of the Press-Bar Committee of the American Society

of Newspaper Editors, 1964–1965, adopted by the ASNE, April 14, 1965.

4. Erwin N. Griswold, "Responsibility of the Legal Profession," address on the Law-Layman Program conducted by the Section of Judicial Administration of the American Bar Association, Waldorf Astoria Hotel, New York, August 11, 1964.

Chapter 12. The Men of Electronic Journalism

1. Ralph Renick, Keynote Address, Radio-Television News Directors Association Annual Conference, Tampa–St. Petersburg, Florida, 1965, as reported in the *RTNDA Bulletin,* November–December, 1965, page 14.

2. KMTV News Department Memorandum 59, dated September 2, 1965.

3. Peter Boultwood, NBC Cameraman, his narration on film report of Vietnam action by the 101st Airborne Division during which Nesson was wounded; aired July 13, 1966, on the Huntley-Brinkley Report.

Chapter 13. What's Ahead in Electronic Journalism

1. Jack Gould, *The New York Times* column, Feb. 13, 1966.

2. Joseph V. Charyk, President of the Communications Satellite Corporation, an address made at the Twentieth Annual Broadcast Engineering Conference, Chicago, Ill., March 28–30, 1966.

3. Jack Gould, *The New York Times* column, Sunday, August 7, 1966.

4. John Schneider, remarks, the National Educational Television program, "At Issue: What's Happening to Television?" No. 65 of a series.

5. William Bluem, *The Documentary in American Television,* Hastings House, 1965, pages 244–45.

6. Willard Schroeder, address, Association for Professional Broadcasting Education luncheon, N. A. B. Convention, Chicago, Ill., March 27, 1966.

INDEX

173

INDEX